GLORIA COP

GOD'S

WILL IS

PROSPERITY

WITH BONUS CONTENT

40TH

ANNIVERSARY
EDITION

God's Will Is Prosperity
40th Anniversary Edition

ISBN 978-1-60463-377-1   30-0579

22 21 20 19 18 17   6 5 4 3 2 1

© 1978 Gloria Copeland

Kenneth Copeland Publications
Fort Worth, TX 76192-0001

For more information about Kenneth Copeland Ministries, call 800-600-7395 or visit www.kcm.org.

CONTENTS

A MESSAGE
FROM GLORIA
COPELAND

Have you ever written a book? Let me tell you what happens when you sit down to write the first word. This morning as I sat down to write *God's Will Is Prosperity*, the first thing I did was look through a folder of notes—little bits and pieces of paper with different scriptures and nuggets from the Word of God—that I have been collecting for several years. One was so old it had turned yellow.

For several years I have known that I would write this book. In fact, I originally intended to include it as the last chapter in my first book, *God's Will for You*. When I finished the other chapters, I tried to write this one, but it seemed that something was missing. I just couldn't get it going. Now I know why. Although I knew some things about the laws of prosperity, I did not have a complete revelation of them. (Of course, you understand that we are still learning in all of these areas.) There were other things about prosperity that I needed to know and walk in before I could share them with you.

Years ago, God said He wanted me to write a book and share what Kenneth and I had learned about living by faith—actually being sustained by our faith in every area of life. He simply wanted me to share with you what He had taught us concerning His will in the new birth, the Holy Spirit, the Word of God, healing, love, and prosperity—a handbook of Christian living. If you have not read *God's Will for You*, I suggest that you do so because it is really the foundation for this book. You could say this is the last chapter.

Faith begins when the will of God is known. Don't be disturbed if you have tried and failed in believing for prosperity. Through God's Word, you can become established and confident that it is indeed the will of God for you to prosper. "Faith cometh by hearing, and hearing by the word of God" (Romans 10:17). As you study, meditate, and receive the scriptures concerning God's will for your prosperity, faith will rise up within you. Just be open and accept God's Word at face value. God does not lie or deceive. He means exactly what He says. He does not *will* one thing and *say* another. God's Word is His will.

This book does not cover the same material as Kenneth's book *The Laws of Prosperity*. I am assuming, for instance, that you are already tithing and operating the basic fundamentals of God's system of prosperity. If you have not studied *The Laws of Prosperity*, you need to do so because without revelation knowledge of tithing and how to worship God with His tithe, you do not have a solid foundation on which to receive the exceedingly great financial promises that God is offering. The very basic beginning of Bible prosperity is tithing.

Tradition teaches that poverty and Christianity are tied together with a very short rope: To be spiritual you *should* suffer want in the material world. *The Word of God simply reveals that lack and poverty are not in line with God's will for the obedient.* Read this book with an open mind and heart. Allow the Holy Spirit to minister the truth to your spirit until you know beyond doubt that *God's Will Is Prosperity.*

GOD'S WILL IS PROSPERITY

In the beginning God placed everything that man could use and enjoy in the Garden. God saw to it that Adam lacked nothing. He lacked no good thing. He was created in the image of God Himself, leaving nothing to be desired.

God furnished Adam with companionship, ability, abundance and a kingdom. He told Adam to be fruitful, multiply, fill the earth, subdue it and have dominion over every living creature. Adam was the master of the Garden, and God was the master of Adam. God's man was free in every way! He knew no bondage until that fatal day when he committed high treason against the Lord God.

The Scriptures tell us that the woman was deceived but the man was not (1 Timothy 2:14). Adam knew that partaking of the tree of knowledge of good and evil meant separation from God. Being fully aware of the consequences, he committed high treason against God and made himself a servant to God's enemy, Satan.

God said, "In the day that you eat, you shall surely die." When Adam partook of the deadly tree, he died, not physically but spiritually. Spiritual death—the nature of Satan—overtook his once-righteous spirit, and he became one with Satan. Sin and death consumed him spiritually. He was *born again* from life to death. Oh, that horrible day when God's creation came under the bondage of corruption and united with Satan, the destroyer. Adam was separated from the Father who is the God of love. Thereafter, he lived under the dominion of Satan whose nature is spiritual death. By his own free will, Adam subjected himself and his kingdom to Satan. Instead of a lord, man became the subject of a merciless and cruel ruler. By natural birth Adam's children—all of mankind—would be born after his new nature of death instead of life, after the nature of Satan instead of God (Romans 5:12, 17).

Every phase of Adam's life came under the curse of his new god, Satan. He was driven from the Garden; abundance was no longer his to enjoy. He had to toil and sweat in order to survive. His beautiful life was overrun by thorns and thistles both in the physical world and in the spiritual world. Sin produced sickness and disease to plague him. Even his wife's nature changed from the nature of God to the nature of Satan. What a catastrophe!

God's will for Adam was abundance and plenty. There was no lack. The Lordship of God provided only good. Poverty and lack came only after Adam changed gods and began to operate under Satan's dominion. Satan is the author of poverty. God is the Author of abundance. When Adam served God, *all* he knew was abundance. He had the best of everything, the crown of life. *God's will for Adam was abundance.* He proved that when He created the Garden of Eden. Since His will does not change, God's will for His people today is abundance (James 1:17).

God's will concerning financial prosperity and abundance is clearly revealed in the Scriptures. From the
beginning of time, He has provided financial prosperity
for His people through obedience to His Word.

It is obvious that God desired Adam to live in abundance, but by Adam's own choice, the lordship of Satan
engulfed man in a curse that resulted in poverty and lack.
God's heart yearns for His people to be free, and through
His infinite wisdom, He has continually provided deliverance for man and freedom from the curse of poverty.

The Blessing of Abraham

And when Abram was ninety years old and nine,
the Lord appeared to Abram, and said unto him,
I am the Almighty God; walk before me, and be
thou perfect [upright]. *And I will make my covenant
between me and thee, and will multiply thee exceedingly.* And Abram fell on his face: and God talked
with him, saying, As for me, behold, my covenant
is with thee, and thou shalt be a father of many
nations. Neither shall thy name any more be called
Abram, but thy name shall be Abraham; for a father
of many nations have I made thee. *And I will make
thee exceeding fruitful,* and I will make nations of
thee, and kings shall come out of thee. *And I will
establish my covenant between me and thee and thy
seed after thee in their generations for an everlasting
covenant, to be a God unto thee, and to thy seed after
thee.* And I will give unto thee, and to thy seed after
thee, the land wherein thou art a stranger, all the
land of Canaan, for an everlasting possession; and
I will be their God. And God said unto Abraham,

Thou shalt keep my covenant therefore, thou, and thy seed after thee in their generations (Genesis 17:1-9).

Look again at verse 7. "And I will establish my covenant between me and thee and thy seed after thee in their generations for an everlasting covenant, to be a God unto thee, and to thy seed after the." I WILL ESTABLISH. The dictionary's definition of *establish* is to "make steadfast, firm or stable; to settle on a firm or permanent basis; to set or fix unalterably." What does this say to you and me? God will make steadfast His covenant with the seed in their generation. God will set, or fix, this covenant with you and me in our day to such a degree that the promise cannot be altered. The promises of the covenant are guaranteed by God. No power can alter God's covenant with you. He will settle His covenant on a permanent basis in your life.

I will be their God. The blessing of God is a powerful force. It took care of Abraham physically and materially and had the promise of spiritual redemption. Abraham was *extremely* rich (Genesis 24:35, AMPC). "The blessing of the Lord, it maketh rich, and he addeth no sorrow with it" (Proverbs 10:22). Genesis 24:1 says, "And Abraham was old, and well stricken in age: and the Lord had blessed Abraham in all things." No enemy could successfully stand before him because he had a covenant with God. God established the covenant in Abraham's generation, and nothing could alter the promise of God because Abraham kept the covenant and walked uprightly before God.

God said He would also establish His covenant with Abraham's seed. "But my covenant will I establish with Isaac" (Genesis 17:21). God said that He would and He did! "And the Lord appeared to him the same night, and said, I am the God of Abraham your father. Fear not, for I am with you and will favor you with blessings and multiply your descendants for the sake of My servant Abraham" (Genesis 26:24, AMPC). The Bible tells us that Isaac "became great and gained more and more until he became very wealthy and distinguished... and the Philistines envied Him" (Genesis 26:13-14, AMPC).

> "THE BLESSING OF THE LORD, IT MAKETH RICH, AND HE ADDETH NO SORROW WITH IT."
>
> Proverbs 10:22

Next, God established Abraham's blessing in Jacob's life. "Thus the man increased and became exceedingly rich, and had many sheep and goats and maidservants, menservants, camels, and donkeys" (Genesis 30:43, AMPC). Jacob's father-in-law deceived and cheated him for years, but that could not alter the covenant (Genesis 31:7-12). Though Jacob crossed over the Jordan with only a staff, he came back as two companies (Genesis 32:10, AMPC). He said, "...for God has dealt graciously with me and I have everything..." Genesis 33:11, AMPC).

Joseph, Jacob's son, was sold into slavery by his brothers, but that did not stop God from establishing His covenant with Joseph in his generation. "But the Lord was with Joseph, and he [though a slave] was a successful and prosperous man; and he was in the house of his master the Egyptian. And his master saw that the Lord was with him, and that the Lord made all that he did to flourish and succeed in his hand" (Genesis 39:2-3, AMPC).

The blessing of the covenant cannot be stopped in the life of an heir of Abraham as long as he keeps the covenant—obeys God and believes that He is able to perform the covenant in his life. *Slavery could not alter the blessing of the covenant.* This would be equivalent to God making a slave in the Old South so prosperous that his owner wanted to partake of his success. What a covenant! It will work under the most adverse circumstances.

Later, the covenant prospered Joseph even in prison. God gave him favor, and the warden put him in charge of the prison. The Lord made whatever Joseph did to prosper (Genesis 39:21-23).

The blessing of the Lord was established in Joseph's life regardless of his circumstances. He came into Egypt as a slave only 13 years before. He was promoted from prison to the office of governor. That was one giant step! God established His covenant with Abraham's seed in Joseph's generation. The Lord gave Joseph favor with Pharaoh, and he made Joseph the governor of Egypt, giving him full charge of the country. "And Pharaoh took off his [signet] ring from his hand and put it on Joseph's hand, and arrayed him in [official] vestments of fine linen and put a gold chain about his neck; he made him to ride in the second chariot which he had, and [officials] cried before him, Bow the knee! And he set him over all the land of Egypt" (Genesis 41:42-43, AMPC).

Because of Abraham, the children of Israel were delivered. "And God heard their sighing and groaning and [earnestly] remembered His covenant with Abraham, with Isaac, and with Jacob" (Exodus 2:24, AMPC). God told Moses, "And I have come down to deliver them out of the hand and power of the Egyptians and to bring them up out of that land to a land good and large, a land flowing with milk and honey [a land of plenty]" (Exodus 3:8,

AMPC). God Himself came down to see about Abraham's descendants because of His covenant with Abraham.

God's dealings with Isaac, Jacob, Joseph, and Moses were the results of the promise He made to establish the covenant with Abraham's seed in their generation. Because of sin, the law of Moses was instituted to meet the needs of Abraham's seed physically and materially until the Messiah would come concerning whom the promise had been made. He would make good the promise of redemption for their spirits.

The blessing and the curse of the law were the results of God's covenant with Abraham. The blessing included *everything* having to do with the physical, material and financial needs. Healing was included in the blessing. Success was included in the blessing. Prosperity was included in the blessing, exceeding financial blessing. If they were obedient to the covenant, they walked in the blessing of Abraham; if they were disobedient, they walked in the curse of the law.

Abraham's blessing was powerful and all-inclusive. God offered him all He had, including His own Son, to pay the penalty for man's treason (Romans 8:32). He literally gave Abraham the resources of heaven and earth. "For when God made [His] promise to Abraham, He swore by Himself, since He had no one greater by whom to swear, saying, Blessing I certainly will bless you and multiplying I will multiply you" (Hebrews 6:13-14, AMPC).

Jesus came because of what God promised to Abraham. "So now we are bringing you the good news (Gospel) that what God promised to our forefathers, this He has completely fulfilled for us, their children, by raising up Jesus" (Acts 13:32-33, AMPC). "For, as we all know, He [Christ] did not take hold of angels [the fallen angels, to give them a helping and delivering hand], but He did take hold of [the fallen] descendants of Abraham [to reach out to them a helping and delivering hand]" (Hebrews 2:16, AMPC). After Jesus paid the price for the rebirth of man's spirit, He went to Abraham's bosom where Abraham and his seed who had died were still waiting for the spiritual fulfillment of the promise, "I will be a God to them" (Luke 16:19-31; Hebrews 2:14-16, AMPC; Ephesians 4:8-10).

The New Covenant, ratified in the blood of Jesus, was the fulfillment of God's promise to Abraham. It is a better covenant than came through Moses, and it rests upon better promises (Hebrews 8:6). The Old Covenant was incomplete as far as man's needs were concerned. It could not change men's hearts; it could only bless them physically and materially (Galatians 3:21).

Christ hath redeemed us from the curse of the law, being made a curse for us...that the blessing of Abraham might come on the Gentiles through Jesus Christ; that we might receive the promise of the Spirit through faith.... For ye are all the children of God by faith in Christ Jesus.... And if ye be Christ's, then are ye Abraham's seed, and heirs according to the promise (Galatians 3:13-14, 26, 29).

Jesus redeemed us from the curse of the law. He paid the penalty for man's sin so that the blessing of Abraham might come on us through Jesus. We through faith receive the promise that God made to Abraham. *Jesus made it possible for you and me to receive Abraham's blessing—God's promise to him.* Through Jesus we have become children of God. We non-Jewish believers fulfill "for a father of many nations have I made thee." Through the sacrifice of Jesus, Abraham became the father of believers of every nationality. "That at that time ye were without Christ, being aliens from the commonwealth of Israel, and strangers from the covenants of promise, having no hope, and without God in the world: But now in Christ Jesus ye who sometimes were far off are made nigh by the blood of Christ" (Ephesians 2:12-13). Without Jesus we would have no promise, no blessing, no covenant, no redemption; but glory to God, we are not without Him!

"And if ye be Christ's, then are ye Abraham's seed, and heirs according to the promise" (Galatians 3:29). We are heirs according to the promise—heirs just as surely as if we were Abraham's descendants by natural birth.

"And I will establish my covenant between me and thee and thy seed after thee in their generations for an everlasting covenant, to be a God unto thee, and to thy seed after thee" (Genesis 17:7). I WILL ESTABLISH. We have seen what the blessing of Abraham produced in the lives of Abraham, Isaac, Jacob and Joseph. The seed of Abraham was as blessed as Abraham. These men were exceedingly wealthy. *Exceedingly* is the biggest word we have, but it does not really express the extent of their wealth. They lived to be old and died satisfied (Genesis 25:8, 35:29). Whatever they did prospered. The covenant of promise could not be stopped in their lives as long as they were upright before God.

"If ye be Christ's, then are ye Abraham's seed and heirs...." "I will establish my covenant between me and thee, and thy seed after thee in their generation." God promised Abraham to establish His covenant with you and me in our generation! We have God's promise as surely as Isaac did. We are both seed and heirs. Because of His promise, God will multiply you exceedingly and make you exceedingly fruitful. God has obligated Himself to bless you as He blessed Abraham. The promise to you is that God will establish His covenant with you in this generation. He has given His Word to prosper you in the same way He prospered Abraham. We have never realized just how great an inheritance Jesus provided for us. It is almost overwhelming; but we are believers, and we can receive this promise by faith. Believe God to establish His covenant with you in your generation.

And beware lest you say in your [mind and] heart, My power and the might of my hand have gotten me this wealth. But you shall [earnestly] remember the Lord your God, for it is He Who gives you power to get wealth, that He may establish His covenant which He swore to your fathers, as it is this day (Deuteronomy 8:17-18, AMPC).

This scripture reveals some important facts:

1. God has given covenant men the power to get wealth.

2. Prosperity, even wealth, is necessary to establish the covenant.

3. In order for God to fulfill what He promised Abraham, He must be allowed to prosper Abraham's descendants *as at this day*—as though today were the day He made the promise.

God's covenant is a covenant of prosperity. His covenant causes prosperity to be manifested in the earth. Psalm 35:27 tells us that God takes pleasure in the prosperity of His men. He cannot establish His covenant in your life without prospering you. The man who holds to poverty rejects the establishment of the covenant. The man who holds to the covenant rejects poverty. Faith in the covenant pleases God. Without faith, it is impossible to please Him.

God's will is to establish His covenant of prosperity in your life and to do it today. "As at this day" means as though He made the agreement with you on this day—today!

The covenant cannot be established in your life unless *you* believe God's Word concerning prosperity. Let there be no doubt about God's will. *God's will is to establish His covenant in the earth.* Prosperity is a major requirement in the establishment of God's will.

God said, "I will establish my covenant." God does not will one thing and promise (say) another. He does not lie or deceive. God's will is to establish His covenant in the earth.

"These are the words of the covenant, which the Lord commanded Moses.... Keep therefore the words of this covenant, and do them, that ye may prosper in all that ye do" (Deuteronomy 29:1, 9). Even under the Old Covenant, physical deliverance and prosperity were no problem for God to bring to pass in the earth. He fully accomplished that part of the blessing under the Old Covenant before Jesus made the supreme sacrifice. Abraham's descendants who kept God's commandment were not just prosperous—they were exceedingly prosperous. It was no challenge to the power of God! Just think how much easier the laws of prosperity will work for us under the New Covenant. We have all the blessings of the Old plus the power of the New! We have been born again with the nature of God. We are one spirit with the Lord. The Greater One lives in us. Jesus has recovered the authority Adam lost because of treason. We are the seed of Abraham in this generation and already enjoy the promise of spiritual deliverance. Our enemy, Satan, has been defeated and put under our feet.

We have been living far below our covenant rights as heirs of the promise. *I am an heir—an heir to the blessing of Abraham!* The world thinks that to become an heir to the Rockefeller fortune would be sensational. Let me tell you, Rockefeller could not begin to buy Abraham!

To be heir to a large estate seems so wonderful—especially to those of us who know of no wealthy relatives! For unearned wealth and riches to simply be handed to you with no strings attached sounds like a dream come true. An heir does not have to work for an inheritance; he just receives it. Someone else works to get it together, and the heir receives the reward of the other person's life.

"And if ye be Christ's, then are ye Abraham's seed, and heirs according to the promise" (Galatians 3:29). You are an heir! Your inheritance is not a certain limited sum of money or real estate—your inheritance is God. You have inherited the resources of God's power and ability to back you and to establish your success in the earth. *He has guaranteed to establish His blessing with you in this generation.* The Scriptures prove that God will go to any length to establish His covenant with Abraham and his descendants. God spared not even His own Son to establish His covenant with Abraham and his seed (Romans 8:32). God is still God. He has changed neither His covenant nor His integrity. His power has not been weakened. He is the covenant-keeping God in our generation. "My covenant will I not break, nor alter the thing that is gone out of my lips" (Psalm 89:34).

You believe in Jesus Christ. You are the seed of Abraham. Abraham's covenant is everlasting. God will establish His covenant with you now in this generation as surely as He did with Abraham, Isaac and Jacob. He has given you Jesus. You have already received the long-awaited redemption of your spirit, so now receive your full inheritance to have all your needs met by God's power— spirit, soul, body, financially and socially. You are an heir!

Don't be like the little girl whose grandfather held out his hand to her with a nickel, a quarter, a half-dollar and a dollar. She took the nickel. She could have taken the dollar. *She could have taken it all!* He was offering it to her.

The Body of Christ has taken the nickel when they could have had the whole handful! We have limited ourselves. When the Church received spiritual redemption, she let go of the rest of the blessing of Abraham. Prosperity and healing became a lost reality. The Church took spiritual blessing and left the prosperity and healing portions of the promise. It is true that spiritual redemption is a greater blessing than prosperity or healing, but God never asked you to choose. God held out His covenant—full of blessings—just as the grandfather held out his hand. He held out the new birth, prosperity and healing. The Church took the new birth and disregarded prosperity and healing.

Praise God, He is still offering us the promise of Abraham—all of it! It has never been altered. All we have to do is take it!

How Abraham Received

For what does the Scripture say? Abraham believed (trusted in) God, and it was credited to his account as righteousness.... For the promise to Abraham or his posterity, that he should inherit the world, did not come through [observing the commands of] the Law but through the righteousness of faith.... Therefore, [inheriting] the promise is the outcome of faith and depends [entirely] on faith, in order that it might be given as an act of grace (unmerited favor), to make it stable and valid and guaranteed to all his descendants—not only to the devotees and adherents of the Law, but also to those who share the faith of Abraham, who is [thus] the father of us all.

As it is written, I have made you the father of many nations. [He was appointed our father] in the sight of God in Whom he believed, Who gives life to the dead and speaks of the nonexistent things that [He has foretold and promised] as if they [already] existed. [For Abraham, human reason for] hope being gone, hoped in faith that he should become the father of many nations, as he had been promised, So [numberless] shall your descendants be. He did not weaken in faith when he considered the [utter] impotence of his own body, which was as good as dead because he was about a hundred years old, or [when he considered] the barrenness of Sarah's [deadened] womb. No unbelief or distrust made him waver (doubtingly question) concerning the promise of God, but he grew strong and was empowered by faith as he gave praise and glory to God, fully satisfied and assured that God was able and mighty to keep His word and to do what He had promised. That is why his faith was credited to him as righteousness (right standing with God). But [the words], It was credited to him, were written not for his sake alone, but [they were written] for our sakes too. [Righteousness, standing acceptable to God] will be granted and credited to us also who believe in (trust in, adhere to, and rely on) God, Who raised Jesus our Lord from the dead, Who was betrayed and put to death because of our misdeeds and was raised to secure our justification (Romans 4:3, 13, 16-25, AMPC).

How did Abraham receive? BY BELIEVING WHAT GOD SAID. The promise did not come to Abraham because of what he did but because of the unmerited favor of God. We are told in this scripture that the promise to inherit the world was dependent entirely on faith—believing what God said. The promise belonged to Abraham, but he had to receive it by faith. He had to believe (trust) that God was able and mighty to keep His Word and do what He had promised. Abraham believed what God had said, even though it looked impossible. He did not consider his body or the deadness of Sarah's womb. He considered what God said to him more powerful than what he saw or felt. *Abraham's faith allowed God to establish the promise in his life.* Abraham's descendants who did not trust the covenant did not walk in the blessing of God's promise. The promise was sure, even while the children of Israel spent 400 years as slaves. They did not depend on the promise, so they did not enjoy the blessings. Man's faith is necessary in order for God to establish His Word in the earth. If the seed is to share the promise of Abraham, the seed must also share the faith of Abraham.

Your faith—believing God's Word instead of what you see—will allow God to establish the promise of Abraham in your life. No unbelief made Abraham waver concerning the promise of God, but he was confident that God was willing and able to do what He had promised.

Abraham knew that it was God's will for him to inherit the world and for him to be multiplied exceedingly. Why? Because God said it. You are in the same position today. God is speaking to you in His Word about your prosperity. He is speaking to you in His Word about your inheritance. He is speaking to you in His Word about being a GOD to you in every area of life. God's will is to bless you exceedingly—beyond any supposed limit—spiritually, physically, mentally, financially and socially.

God operates by promise. He gives His Word to bless a man, and that promise (the Word) has to be believed and trusted. We call this faith. I believe God's promise. I keep His covenant. I expect it to be in my life even as He promised to Abraham.

For God to establish His covenant (His will) in your life, *you* must believe what He says to *you* in His Word. "And God said unto Abraham, Thou shalt keep my covenant therefore, thou, and thy seed after thee in their generations" (Genesis 17:9).

GOD'S WILL IS PROSPERITY!

PRIORITIES

D o not gather and heap up and store up for yourselves treasures on earth, where moth and rust and worm consume and destroy, and where thieves break through and steal. But gather and heap up and store for yourselves treasures in heaven, where neither moth nor rust nor worm consume and destroy, and where thieves do not break through and steal; for where your treasure is, there will your heart be also.

The eye is the lamp of the body. So if your eye is sound, your entire body will be full of light. But if your eye is unsound, your whole body will be full of darkness. If then the very light in you [your conscience] is darkened, how dense is that darkness!

No one can serve two masters; for either he will hate the one and love the other, or he will stand by and be devoted to the one and despise and be against the other. You cannot serve God and mammon (deceitful riches, money, possessions or what is trusted in).

> "BUT SEEK (AIM AT AND STRIVE AFTER) FIRST OF ALL HIS RIGHTEOUSNESS (HIS WAY OF DOING AND BEING RIGHT), AND THEN ALL THESE THINGS TAKEN TOGETHER WILL BE GIVEN YOU BESIDES."
>
> Matthew 6:33, AMPC

Therefore I tell you, stop being perpetually uneasy (anxious and worried) about your life, what you shall eat or what you shall drink; or about your body, what you shall put on. Is not life greater [in quality] than food, and the body [far above and more excellent] than clothing? Look at the birds of the air; they neither sow nor reap nor gather into barns, and yet your heavenly Father keeps feeding them. Are you not worth much more than they?

And who of you by worrying and being anxious can add one unit of measure (cubit) to his stature or to the span of his life? And why should you be anxious about clothes? Consider the lilies of the field and learn thoroughly how they grow; they neither toil nor spin. Yet I tell you, even Solomon in all his magnificence (excellence, dignity, and grace) was not arrayed like one of these. But if God so clothes the grass of the field, which today is alive and green and tomorrow is tossed into the furnace, will He not much more surely clothe you, O you of little faith?

Therefore do not worry and be anxious, saying, What are we going to have to eat? or, What are we going to have to drink? or, What are we going to have to wear? For the Gentiles (heathen) wish for and crave and diligently seek all these things, and your heavenly Father knows well that you need them all.

But seek (aim at and strive after) first of all His kingdom and His righteousness (His way of doing and being right), and then all these things taken together will be given you besides (Matthew 6:19-33, AMPC).

In these scriptures Jesus is teaching His disciples. The subject is how to handle material things such as treasures, riches, possessions, food, drink and clothes. This broad spectrum begins with the bare necessities and extends to the abundance of possessions. Let's study these scriptures and see what we can learn.

It is obvious throughout the Bible that God is not against a man having money. God's covenant men were the wealthiest men of their day. They were God's men and He was pleased with them. Their attitude toward God's Word allowed Him to establish His covenant with them in their generation. God is the One who gave them the power to get wealth. "And beware lest you say in your [mind and] heart, My power and the might of my hand have gotten me this wealth. But you shall [earnestly] remember the Lord your God, for it is He Who gives you power to get wealth, that He may establish His covenant which He swore to your fathers, as it is this day" (Deuteronomy 8:17-18, AMPC). No, God is not against a man having money. He is against money having the man. He is not opposed to His people being rich, but He is opposed to them being covetous.

Jesus says not to gather, heap up and store for yourselves treasures on earth. "And he said unto them, Take heed, and beware of covetousness: for a man's life consisteth not in the abundance of the things which he possesseth" (Luke 12:15). In Luke 12:21, He speaks about the man who continues to lay up, or hoard, possessions for himself and is not rich toward God. To hoard is not of God. Evidently, the man was not remembering that it was God who had given him the power to get wealth. (Your affection is not to be in your prosperity, business, goods, treasures or holdings.) Jesus said this rich man had fertile land which yielded so plentifully that he had a problem. He was in a dilemma. All of his storehouses were full, and he did not have room to store another big harvest, so he decided to tear down his storehouses and build bigger ones. Then he said, "Now I have good things laid up for many years. I can just live the way I want to." (Where was his trust? In the things he had laid up, the things he had hoarded!)

"But God said to him, You fool! This very night they [the messengers of God] will demand your soul of you; and all the things that you have prepared, whose will they be? So it is with the one who continues to lay up and hoard possessions for himself and is not rich [in his relation] to God [this is how he fares]" (Luke 12:20-21, AMPC). Trusting in riches will go only as far as the riches will go. Money can buy only so much, and it can leave your possession very fast! God's prosperity reaches into every area of a man's life.

Ken's definition of *true prosperity* is "the ability to use the power of God to meet the needs of mankind." If a man needs healing, money will not help him. If his body is well but he has no money to pay the rent, God's healing power will not cover his need. God is so generous with us that He desires His children to have the best in life on earth, just as you desire the best for your children. God's plan for us is to have *all* of our needs met according to His riches in glory by Christ Jesus. True prosperity is having every need met.

God's laws of prosperity carry with them a built-in protection. For His laws of prosperity to work in your life, you must be spiritually ready to prosper. Throughout the Bible, God's people prospered when they obeyed His Word; but when they were disobedient, His laws of prosperity did not work for them. They were still His people, but His powerful blessing was not manifested in their lives. "Keep therefore the words of this covenant, and do them, that ye may prosper in all that ye do" (Deuteronomy 29:9). God does not change. The laws of prosperity will work in the life of any person who is obedient to His Word.

You will not prosper by believing only the part of God's Word concerning material blessing. If your motive is to be prosperous without serving God, you had better read some other book. God's prosperity will work only in the life of the believer who is committed to the Word because he loves God—not for material gain.

YOUR FIRST PRIORITY IS TO PLEASE GOD. For where your treasure is, there will your heart be also. If your treasure is Jesus as Lord and the Word of God as the lamp unto your feet, then you are a candidate for the material blessings of God.

In the sixth chapter of Matthew, Jesus explains the saying, "The eye is the lamp of the body." Yes, He is still teaching about treasures, possessions and material goods.

You have to start with your priorities in the right place. Then, when you begin to enjoy material prosperity, you must be sure to keep your priorities in line.

The eye is the lamp of the body. If your eye is sound, your body is sound. Look at Proverbs 4:20-22, AMPC, "My son, attend to my words; consent and submit to my sayings. Let them not depart from your sight; keep them in the center of your heart. For they are life to those who find them, healing and health to all their flesh." Solomon, the wisest and richest man of any day, gave these instructions again in Proverbs 7:2, "Keep my commandments, and live; and my law as the apple of thine eye." The apple, or pupil, is the center of your eye. The sound eye stays on the Word of God. This is how you keep sound though materially prosperous. You are to keep your eye on God's Word—not on money or possessions. Jesus explains why in Matthew 6:24: You cannot serve two masters. You cannot serve God and mammon. If you put your eye on, or give attention to, riches and material possessions, you will begin to serve them instead of them serving you. You are supposed to keep your eye (your attention) on God's Word and serve Him. You cannot keep your eye in both places. You cannot serve two masters; Jesus said so. You will be devoted to one and be against the other. So the line is drawn and there is no middle ground.

"If ye then be risen with Christ, seek those things which are above, where Christ sitteth on the right hand of God. Set your affection on things above, not on things on the earth" (Colossians 3:1-2). We are instructed to seek those things which are above! *We are to set our affections.* You are to set your mind on things above and refuse to allow money or possessions to control your thinking and actions. You set your affections to serve God, not riches.

Mark 4:18-19 reveals why it is imperative that we set our affections on the things of God instead of on the things of the earth. "And these are they which are sown among thorns; such as hear the word, and the cares of this world, and the deceitfulness of riches, and the lusts of other things entering in, choke the word, and it becometh unfruitful."

If your affection is set on wealth and riches instead of God, the Word becomes unfruitful in your life. Covetousness chokes the Word. The Word cannot bear fruit in a man who has his affections set on the things of the earth. The successful faith man sets his mind (affection) on the Word of God. You cannot serve God and mammon. You will serve one or the other. Jesus said to "beware of covetousness." It is a tool of Satan to render God's Word powerless in your life. Refuse to allow your affection to be on your possessions, business, treasures and holdings. Demand that your affections be set on God's Word. Make an irrevocable decision to serve God's Word and give it first place in your life. Set your affection on things that are above. Your spiritual life will be intact, *and* all other things will be yours to enjoy as well. The possessions that are added to you will serve you instead of you serving them.

The choice is yours as to which you serve. Either you will trust in mammon (deceitful riches, money, possessions) or you will trust in God. If you trust in mammon, when you are instructed by God to give a large amount into His work, you will give a small amount instead, saying, "I would like to give more, but it is all tied up." You are serving the riches. That is where you have placed your faith.

But if your eye is single on God's Word and He instructs you to give, you will say, "You know that my money is tied up, so at Your instruction, praise the Lord, I will untie it." The man whose eye is single on the Word knows that when he gives, it shall be given to him again—not just the amount he gave but good measure, pressed down, shaken together, and running over (Luke 6:38). He is not hoarding. He is ready to distribute as God tells him. He is not trusting in his riches. He has his confidence in God's ability to put him over. Money is his servant. He does not serve money. He serves God. This is a man who is rich toward God.

Trust

In Matthew 6:25, Jesus tells us that we are to have an attitude of trust and faith concerning material things. He says to STOP being anxious and worried over things (food, clothes, material possessions). Don't try to figure out how God is going to meet your needs. Be like the birds of the air and know that your heavenly Father is taking care of you. STOP being worried. Do not seek after these things like the ungodly do. Why? Because we have a Father. We have a covenant with God. Their father, Satan, does not look after them; but our Father knows what we have need of, and He delights in providing for us (Psalm 35:27). What a blessing!

Jesus not only tells us what not to seek, but He goes on to tell us what we are to seek. We are not to be idle. There is something we are to do: SEEK FIRST OF ALL HIS KINGDOM AND HIS RIGHTEOUSNESS. How do you do that? By the Word of God. *Give the Word first place in your life.* Commit yourself to obey whatever you see in the Word.

Kenneth and I made that very commitment years ago when we first began to find out how faith works. We agreed then that we would do whatever we saw in God's Word. Without even knowing it, we had placed ourselves in position to receive great financial blessings. Our desire was to please God. We were committed to His Word. We didn't know how to believe God for material things. We didn't even know that the instructions in God's Word will *always work to our advantage*—even in this life. But had we known that we would never *increase* financially, we would still have acted the very same way.

When we first learned that God would meet our needs, we were living in Tulsa, Oklahoma, where Kenneth was enrolled in Oral Roberts University. We desired to please God with all of our hearts, and we had moved out in what little faith we knew.

Financially, times were hard. I really think that we were *supernaturally* in debt! No matter how hard we tried, we couldn't get out of debt. We just seemed to get in deeper and deeper. Let's face it, borrowed money was our source. After we paid the bills, there was no money left for anything else. Old obligations were left unpaid, and there was threat of a lawsuit. I can remember standing in the checkout line at the grocery store, praying in the spirit, and believing God that I had enough money to pay for the groceries in my basket. Whatever I had in my purse at the time was all we had!

We didn't know then what we know now about operating in the laws of prosperity. We were just beginning to learn about the integrity of the Word. You can depend on God's Word in the same way that you depend on the word of a doctor, a lawyer, or your very best friend. We knew that the Word of God never fails, and we had committed to do whatever we saw in the Word, no matter what it was.

Then we saw Romans 13:8, "Owe no man any thing, but to love one another." *Surely God didn't mean that! That scripture must mean something else.* Another translation says, "KEEP OUT OF DEBT AND OWE NO MAN ANYTHING."

As Satan told Eve in the Garden, we thought, "Can it really be that God said, 'Owe no man anything'? *There must be some other explanation.*" We found out that there were indeed other explanations, but somehow they didn't ring true.

People who knew more than we did said things like, "Well, you don't owe anybody until the payment is due." Tell that to your banker the next time you apply for a loan. "I really don't owe that $8,000 listed as a liability for my car because I have already made my payment this month."

We wanted to be convinced. It looked impossible to do anything without borrowing money. We had never considered paying cash for a car. We had never bought furniture. *How would we ever have anything?* The material possession I wanted most in the world was a home. *Pay cash for a house? You must be kidding!* Satan would say, "You will never get it." We actually did not know that we could receive all these things with our faith. As far as we knew then, we might never be able to have the finer things in life.

Yes, we had a choice, but not a good one as far as we could tell then. We had said, "We are taking God's Word literally, and whatever we see in it, that's what we will do." But when we made that commitment, we did not know it said, "KEEP OUT OF DEBT." The other choice was to continue operating in the manner we always had and explain away Romans 13:8. *That verse must not mean what it says. To live well without borrowing money would be impossible.* (Notice the word *well*. You know you could live, but it's the "living well" that hurts the flesh!)

Praise the Lord! We had already set our affections on the Word of God. Our commitment to obey God's Word won out over circumstances, people and Satan. We made the decision to take Romans 13:8 for just what it says. We stopped using our charge accounts and began to believe God to get out of debt. As far as we knew at the time, we might never have anything more than we had right then (which, believe me, was not much). Everything we had ever bought was "buy now, pay later"—sometimes it was much later than they thought!

I don't think anybody could have started further down than we did, especially considering that we had no steady income; but we were determined to walk according to what we saw in the Word. Our affections were set. Things were slow in the beginning, but we knew that there must be a way, and we were determined to find that way and walk in it. Under some circumstances you can learn very fast, and we had left ourselves only one way to go—God's way. Things didn't come to us in one day. We had to build the Word of God into our spirits and walk in what we knew. We would get some of the Word in us and walk in it, get more Word in us and walk in that, and get more Word and walk in that.

We were involved with the Word almost every waking hour. Television was not interesting to us. We could not have told you what movies were showing. Even world events could not hold our attention. Literally night and day, we were devoted to God's Word. We did not make a decision to do away with television; we just had no time for it. We were so thrilled with the Word of God that there was nothing else as exciting. We were fulfilling Joshua 1:8, "This Book of the Law shall not depart out of your mouth, but you shall meditate on it day and night, that you may observe and do according to all that is written in it. For then you shall make your way prosperous, and then you shall deal wisely and have good success" (AMPC).

When we started believing God to get out of debt, we did it uncompromisingly. We were committed to the Word regardless and were not willing to borrow money. Yes, many times through the years we have been encouraged to borrow. Yes, we know most people think we are extreme, and no doubt we are, but the Word of God will produce just as far as you dare to commit to it. We have done everything God has instructed us to do to expand our ministry. We have always had the very best provided for us. We have been able to do whatever we wanted to do. The Word of God has been our source—not financial institutions. In the beginning we were faithful over little, but in the end God made us ruler over much (Luke 16:10). God has never loaned us anything. He has always given to us. We are convinced that this was the greatest decision we have ever made, other than making Jesus Christ the Lord of our lives.

Yes! You could say that we are extreme. We are *extremely* free! (Remember, Abraham was extreme: he was *extremely* rich!) That decision opened the door of freedom for us. We committed to the Word, and the Word made us free.

Examine what we did in the light of the scriptures we are studying. Without knowing it, we were doing the right thing. We were putting first things first: keeping our eyes single on the Word of God. We did not allow possessions or the lack of them to get our attention. We did not try to serve two masters. We served only God's Word. We were not trusting in money, we were trusting in the Word. We were too thrilled with the Word of God to be worried or anxious about anything. In short, WE WERE SEEKING FIRST THE KINGDOM OF GOD AND HIS RIGHTEOUSNESS.

We didn't know from experience that we could live a prosperous life, but we did know Romans 13:8. We were committed to get out of debt because we saw that particular thing in the Word. That was our only motive. We were not doing these things in order to become prosperous. Actually, we were operating scripturally.

We had taken the first step into God's prosperity by seeking first His kingdom according to Matthew 6:33. Then all the other things were added to us. If you could just pick out certain portions of the Word and live by them, it would be a dangerous situation. You cannot simply decide to take the promise of prosperity from God's Word and live by that, ignoring the part about living a dedicated life before God. You may try it, but it won't work for you if you are not seeking first the kingdom of God. The eye is not single. It is not on the Word but on material blessing.

Third John 2 says, "Beloved, I wish above all things that thou mayest prosper and be in health, even as thy soul prospereth." In other words, you will prosper to the degree that your soul prospers. Bible prosperity will not come any other way. The laws of prosperity are based on obedience to God's Word. That is the built-in protection of the laws of prosperity.

It was 11 months from the time that we first decided to believe God to get out of debt until that goal was achieved. During those 11 months, we stood fast on what we knew from God's Word. We began to learn the revelation knowledge that we operate in now: how to live by faith, how to use faith, how faith comes, and how it works.

Your faith may not be developed to the place where you can "owe no man anything but to love him." Being free from debt and obligation is God's best for us, but most people have not developed enough to maintain the walk. It is not an easy thing in a world that operates on borrowed money.

Divine healing without any outside help—doctors or medicine—is God's best, but many are not able to receive by faith alone. Until you are able to live in divine health, go to the doctor in faith. It is not a sin to take medicine or go to the doctor, although it is more blessed to have need of neither. The same is true of borrowing money. Living a life free of debt is possible and desirable, but your faith will have to be developed to enjoy that blessing.

Just begin to believe God where you are. You can only operate on the level of your own faith. But faith grows as you study God's Word and apply it.

When people ask, "Should I have this operation or should I stand on the Word?" my answer is, "If you have to ask, you better see the doctor."

Feed on the scriptures concerning prosperity and the generosity and goodness of God until your faith is alive and ready to believe God for any need you might have.

DIVINE
PROSPERITY

The first thing I began to believe God for was a home. *But what about Romans 13:8? It says that we are to owe no man anything but to love him. How can you believe God for enough money to buy a home?* This is one area most people think impossible. Many have made the statement, "Surely you don't have to believe for a home without borrowing money!"

You certainly don't have to, but I happen to know it works. Of course, Satan told me that there was no way I could have a home without borrowing money for it. That is the world's way and what everyone is expected to do, but I refused to believe Satan. We had made an irrevocable commitment—we were not going to borrow money. Believing God was the *only way* I could have my home.

When Satan would come at me with doubt and unbelief, this is one verse I trusted in. I confessed it continually, and it gave me comfort and strength to stand in faith. Second Corinthians 9:8, AMPC, says, "And God is able to make all grace (every favor and earthly blessing) come to you in abundance, so that you may always and under all

> "AND GOD IS ABLE TO MAKE ALL GRACE (EVERY FAVOR AND EARTHLY BLESSING) COME TO YOU IN ABUNDANCE, SO THAT YOU MAY ALWAYS AND UNDER ALL CIRCUMSTANCES AND WHATEVER THE NEED BE SELF-SUFFICIENT [POSSESSING ENOUGH TO REQUIRE NO AID OR SUPPORT AND FURNISHED IN ABUNDANCE FOR EVERY GOOD WORK AND CHARITABLE DONATION]."
>
> 2 Corinthians 9:8
> *AMPC*

circumstances and whatever the need be self-sufficient [possessing enough to require no aid or support and furnished in abundance for every good work and charitable donation]."

Satan would come at me with thoughts of doubt and say, "There is no way you are going to have your needs met. There is no way you can buy a house without going into debt. There is just no way!" I would answer him with, "No, Satan, my God is able!" *I hung my faith on that scripture.*

The Word says that He is able to get it to you. Don't look to natural sources. Don't look to your job. When you are believing God, you have to look to His Word. KEEP YOUR EYE SINGLE ON THE WORD. You have to realize and know that He can and will work in your behalf. God is a real operator! He is ABLE to get things done!

So, we started believing God years ago for the home we have now. We could have borrowed the money years sooner, but we refused to compromise on our decision. Whenever there is a choice between the world's way and the Word's way, we always go with the Word. The world's system may seem to be the easier way, but we refuse to go the way of the world. In the long run, God's way is not only easier but far superior. He has certainly proven that to us.

We began believing God for the perfect home when we lived in Tulsa, Oklahoma, in 1968. At the same time, there was a lady in Forth Worth, Texas, who started building her home. She had the plans drawn and saw to the purchasing of materials personally. It was several years before I saw that home, but the floor plan was exactly what we needed to meet our needs as a family. In addition to the living space, there was a study in the back of the house—a place away from the living area where we could study the Word and write. It was perfect for us. *She began to build it at the very time we began to believe for it!*

God started to work immediately. There was no evidence of that for us to see, but we had learned to look to the Word for evidence and not to the circumstances.

When we first looked at the house, we were on our way to the airport to leave town. Really, at first I didn't know exactly what I had in mind. As I thought about the house over the next few days, the Lord started showing me things I could do to it. The house had stayed empty for months. It seemed that nobody could live there. The owners were just trying to get rid of it. They had given it away once but got it back. They couldn't even give it away! That was our home!

When I believe God for something, I don't waver. I have made a quality decision that the Word is true. I have built into myself a reliance on God's Word. I believe His Word more than I believe what I can see or feel. I know that God is able and He will get it to me. As I have heard

Kenneth Hagin say, "If you are determined to stand forever, it won't take very long." That's the way I am when I am believing God for something. I could stand forever if necessary.

We leased the house for one year. We agreed to pay cash for it at the end of that year. Our needs had always been met abundantly. We lived well. We did what we wanted to do. But as far as having that much money in cash, we just didn't have it and never had. In the natural there was no reason to expect to have it, but in the spirit we knew our God was able. When we moved in, the house was in need of repair. It needed to be completely remodeled, so I was faced with a decision. I had enough money to start the remodeling because I had saved some money to buy a home when I found one; but I thought, *This is not our home legally. It would really be unwise to put thousands of dollars into a house that doesn't even belong to us.* What was I supposed to do? At that point, I had to act on my faith. I decided that it was my house—I had believed that I received it. I had put my foot on that place, and it was mine in the Name of Jesus. As an act of faith, I went to work, calling in people to start remodeling. During that year Satan said, "Well, that sure is a lot of money for you to lose."

But I would answer, "No, in the Name of Jesus, this is my house and it will be paid for in July. We will pay cash for it. I believe we have the money in the Name of Jesus!"

Whenever God called us to do something in the ministry, we always had to believe Him for the money before we could start. Because we wouldn't borrow money, we had to wait until we had the cash. When we went into television, we believed God for the money first before we actually started production. In the radio ministry, we did the same thing. We might have to believe God for six months before the money would come into our hands. That is how we had always operated. During that year, the ministry was growing and stretching out; the payroll was growing. We always had enough to meet the budget, but it was *nip and tuck*. There never was anything much left over.

Paying cash for a home is a challenge to faith. We had by faith stepped into a situation that certainly was beyond our natural ability or means. We were trusting the Word of God to perform and accomplish our goal, and the Word came to our rescue with further revelation! We were committed to God's Word, and God was committed to us. We had taken the step of faith, and God saw to it that we had the revelation knowledge of His Word to put us over. I am convinced beyond doubt that our commitment years before to stay out of debt made the difference. If we had not committed to God's Word then, we would not know what we know today about God's system of finance. We would not be able to share these things with you, and today we would be living far below our privileges as believers.

A Divine Revelation

One day as I was standing in my house looking out the window and thinking about these things, God gave me what I would call a revelation of *divine prosperity*. I realized that we had been looking at finances and prosperity in a different way from other things, such as divine health. If a symptom of sickness came on my body, I would not stand for it. I would take authority over it immediately and not allow it to remain. By doing this, I walk in divine health. I am convinced that healing and divine health belong to me in the New Covenant.

Divine prosperity works exactly the same way, but we had not been using the Word to believe for divine prosperity as we had for divine health. We had been living in the laws of prosperity for years, but we had been acting on prosperity differently from other provisions of the Word in this way: *We would allow symptoms of lack to come on us and stay there. We were willing to tolerate them.* When the Lord began to deal with me on this, He made me realize that Jesus bore the curse of poverty at the same time He bore the curse of sickness. I already knew it, but I saw that I was not acting on it to the fullest. You can believe for divine prosperity just as you believe for divine health. Both blessings already belong to you. You should refuse lack just as quickly as you refuse sickness.

There was a time when we knew that praying for the sick was a valid thing. When we got sick, we would pray, and most of the time we would get healed. We knew that healing was for us. We knew it was real, so we believed God for healing when we got sick. But when we heard through Kenneth Hagin that Jesus bore our sicknesses and carried our diseases and by His stripes we were healed, the situation was changed in our lives concerning healing. We didn't wait until we got sick to believe God for healing. We decided to walk in divine health because we *were* healed 2,000 years ago when Jesus paid the price.

I remember the night we heard that we *were* healed by the stripes of Jesus. We realized then that we didn't have to be sick anymore. Getting healed when you are sick is great, but staying healed—walking in divine health—is much greater. To get healed is wonderful, but it is much better to realize that Jesus paid for our sicknesses and that we are free from them. He made us free from sickness, and Satan cannot put anything on us without our consent. It may be a consent of ignorance, but nevertheless, you are willing to let him do it. He can't affect you unless you let him.

Jesus paid the price for your sickness. It is not a promise. It is a fact. It has already been done. We need to see prosperity in the same light that we see healing and health. He bore the curse of poverty. We should always have enough. Jesus provided it for us. If you are in lack, if you don't have enough to get by, if you don't have anything extra to invest in the work of the gospel, then you are in an area of poverty—you are suffering symptoms of lack.

Isaiah 1:19 says, "If ye be willing and obedient, ye shall eat the good of the land." The word *willing* has become a passive word in our thinking. Actually, in this scripture *willing* is an action word. It involves a decision. If I said, "I am *willing* to live in divine health," I wouldn't just mean, "Well, if somebody slaps it on me, I'll live in it." No. If I am *willing*, I have made up my mind to live that way. I have determined, "I *will* live in divine health. I'm not *willing* to be sick."

If you make up your mind—make a quality decision—that you are not willing to live in lack but that you are willing to live in divine prosperity and abundance, Satan cannot stop the flow of God's financial blessings. If you are willing and obedient, you shall eat the good of the land. Divine prosperity will come to pass in your life. You have exercised your faith in the covenant that you have with God. You have opened the door for Him to establish His covenant with you.

It takes the same kind of decision regarding divine prosperity that it takes for divine health. *To walk in divine health, you begin with a decision to no longer allow Satan to put sickness on you;* and Satan loses dominion over your body. Frankly, I am just not willing to be sick. I am willing to be well! Jesus paid the price for me, and I am taking advantage of it. In honor of His sacrifice, I will not accept anything less than divine health.

In the same way, I am not *willing* to live in lack. If I thought abundance was not in agreement with God's will, or if I thought that the Word of God did not provide abundance, I would simply leave it alone. But the Word does provide prosperity and abundance for me. I am an heir to the blessing of Abraham. Redemption from the curse of poverty is part of Jesus' substitutionary work at Calvary. He paid the price for my prosperity—a heavy price. I will not scorn any part of His work. I deeply appreciate every benefit that His sacrifice provided for me.

Once you make the decision to receive what Jesus has already provided for you and to walk in Bible prosperity, Satan cannot stop you from being prosperous. When you made the decision to make Jesus the Lord of your life according to Romans 10:9-10, there was no devil in hell that could stop your salvation from coming to pass. Satan and all of his cohorts could not even slow it down. Salvation was being offered; and when you made the decision to receive it, salvation immediately became yours and you became a new creature in Christ Jesus. There was no struggle. Salvation was offered and you took it! So it is with Bible prosperity. *You begin to walk in divine prosperity with a decision to no longer allow Satan to put symptoms of lack on you.*

Make this quality decision concerning your prosperity: *God's blessing of prosperity belongs to me. I WILL receive it. The symptoms of lack have no right to operate against me.*

Make this decision and you will begin to enjoy the financial blessing that has belonged to you since you became a believer in Jesus Christ.

Redeemed From the Curse

Deuteronomy 28 describes the curse of the law. You can see from these verses that poverty is included in this curse: "And you shall grope at noonday as the blind grope in darkness. And you shall not prosper in your ways; and you shall be only oppressed and robbed continually, and there shall be no one to save you...you shall build a house, but not live in it.... A nation which you have not known shall eat up the fruit of your land and of all your labors, and you shall be only oppressed and crushed continually.... He [the stranger] shall lend to you, but you shall not lend to him; he shall be the head, and you shall be the tail. All these curses shall come upon you and shall pursue you and overtake you" (Deuteronomy 28:29-30, 33, 44-45, AMPC).

From these verses we can plainly see that poverty and lack are a part of the curse of the law. Galatians 3:13-14 very simply says, "Christ hath redeemed us from the curse of the law, being made a curse for us: for it is written, Cursed is every one that hangeth on a tree: That the blessing of Abraham might come on the Gentiles through Jesus Christ." The blessing of Abraham definitely included a financial blessing. The curse of the law definitely included financial reversal.

Galatians 3:13 is one of the verses that caused healing to be a reality in our lives. We knew beyond a doubt that sickness and disease were under the curse and that healing was a part of the blessing of Abraham. Now we can use the same scripture to make divine prosperity a reality in our lives. Jesus redeemed us from the curse of poverty. He redeemed us from every curse of the law.

If we are willing and obedient, the blessing of Abraham will come on us and overtake us. God will multiply us exceedingly and make us exceedingly fruitful. Lack should be a thing of the past, and abundance—more than you can see any way to use—should be the order of the day.

Peace and Prosperity

Another scripture that has meant so much to us with regard to healing is Isaiah 53:5, AMPC: "But He was wounded for our transgressions, He was bruised for our guilt and iniquities; the chastisement [needful to obtain] peace and well-being for us was upon Him, and with the stripes [that wounded] Him we are healed and made whole." This says that Jesus bore the *chastisement needful to obtain peace and well-being*. Peace and well-being include whatever you need. You can't enjoy peace and well-being if you don't have your needs met. Isaiah 48:18, AMPC, ties the two together, "Oh, that you had hearkened to My commandments! Then your peace and prosperity would have been like a flowing river." Peace and well-being include a prosperous life. God told Abram, "Fear not, Abram, I am your Shield, your abundant compensation, and your reward shall be exceedingly great" (Genesis 15:1, AMPC). Abundant compensation is far-reaching. Abundant compensation means everything. It enveloped Abraham in a blanket of well-being.

Peace and prosperity go hand in hand. Your prosperity has already been provided for you. I pray this will become a reality to you today. Prosperity is yours! It is not something you have to strive to work toward. YOU HAVE A TITLE DEED TO PROSPERITY. Jesus bought and paid for your prosperity just as He bought and paid for your healing and your salvation. He bore the curse of sin, of sickness, and of poverty. When He paid the price for sin, He also paid the price for the curse of poverty so that you can be free.

Once you realize that this prosperity *already* belongs to you, you will be in a different position. You will no longer be seeking to obtain it, hoping to get it, or working toward it. You won't have to work toward it because the Word says it is yours now. The Word is your source in prosperity just as it is in healing.

Treat any symptom of lack just as you would treat a symptom of sickness. The very moment a symptom of lack shows up in your life, take authority over it. Command it to flee from you in the Name of Jesus and stand your ground. Say, "Lack, I resist you in the Name of Jesus. I command you to flee from me. I have been redeemed from the curse of poverty and lack. I WILL NOT TOLERATE YOU IN MY LIFE." Don't allow Satan to steal from you. He will attempt to put symptoms of lack on you, but if you stand on the Word of God, knowing that prosperity belongs to you, he cannot maintain an attack. The Word says that when you resist Satan, he has to flee from you. He has no choice (James 4:7)!

Dominion

Divine prosperity and abundance belong to you now. We, as born-again believers, have the same authority over the earth that Adam had in the Garden of Eden. Look at Genesis 1:27-28, AMPC: "So God created man in His own image, in the image and likeness of God He created him; male and female He created them. And God blessed them and said to them, Be fruitful, multiply, and fill the earth, and subdue it [using all its vast resources in the service of God and man]; and have dominion over the fish of the sea, the birds of the air, and over every living creature that moves upon the earth." God made the earth, and then He made man and gave man dominion and authority over the earth. It was man's earth (Psalm 115:16). God didn't say, "I will subdue it for you." He said, "You subdue it and have dominion over its vast resources."

While we were standing in faith for the money to pay for our first house, the Lord reminded me of this scripture and revealed to me that every material thing here came from the earth's vast resources. Every piece of lumber, brick, glass, concrete, mortar—there was nothing in the makeup of our house that had not come from the earth's resources. *Be fruitful, multiply, and fill the earth, and subdue it with all its vast resources and have dominion.* Anything that you can see with your eyes comes from the earth's resources. (I had not thought about that even though it is obvious that it does.) Every jet airplane is made from material that comes from the earth's resources. Cars, buildings, furniture, jewels, food, clothes, every greenback dollar bill, silver and gold are products of the earth's vast resources. You cannot have a material need that the earth's resources cannot handle. The raw materials may change, but the substance that gives material things their form comes from the resources of the earth! Glory to God!

God told Adam to subdue the earth and its resources. He gave Adam authority over it. Adam gave that authority to Satan. Then Jesus came to earth, paid the price, and recaptured that authority from Satan. Jesus, in turn, gave that authority to the believer. "And Jesus came and spake unto them, saying, All power is given unto me in heaven and in earth. Go ye therefore, and teach all nations, baptizing them in the name of the Father, and of the Son, and of the Holy Ghost: Teaching them to observe all things whatsoever I have commanded you: and, lo, I am with you always, even unto the end of the world" (Matthew 28:18-20).

I began to see that I already had authority over that house and authority over the money I needed to purchase it. I said, "In the Name of Jesus, I take authority over the money I need. (I called for the specific amount.) I command you to come to me. I take my place, and I take dominion over that which I need. I command it to come in Jesus'. Name. Ministering spirits, you go and cause it to come." (Speaking of angels, Hebrews 1:14 says, "Are they not all ministering spirits, sent forth to minister for them who shall be heirs of salvation?" You have angels assigned to minister for you. Psalm 103:20 says that the angels hearken to the voice of God's Word. When you become the voice of God in the earth by putting His Words in your mouth, you put your angels to work! They are highly trained, capable helpers. They know how to get the job done.)

I wasn't taking authority over something that belonged to someone else. That house was up for sale. The people had relinquished their authority when they put it on the market. I had the right to take authority over it and receive it as mine in the Name of Jesus.

Stand your ground on the Word of God simply because it is yours. Believe it and the things you need will come into your life. Take authority over them and command them to come to you in the Name of Jesus. Command the money you need to come to you. The authority is yours. Have dominion and subdue the earth and its vast resources.

Mark 10:29-30 tells us a hundredfold return is available to the giver, but it says that you will receive your return "with persecutions." Persecution simply means that Satan will try you. Persecution has no authority over you. It has no power, but Satan is allowed to test you in that area. He will lie to you and steal from you if he can. He will show you convincing symptoms of lack and tell you, "There is no way." Remember those four words *there is no way* always come from Satan. God will never tell you there is no way. Jesus said, "I am the way." The only way to successfully combat Satan is with the Word of God and the Name of Jesus.

It was six years from the time we started believing God for our first home until we moved into it. At the end of the year's lease, we paid cash for our "faith house." I am still not sure how, except by faith in God's Word. Had we borrowed the money, we would have still had 35 years to pay! When you think about that, six years does not seem so long. Remember that in 1968 we had hardly scratched the surface of revelation knowledge. We had just realized that faith works. We did not know *how* God's system of prosperity worked. Since then we have learned and are still learning. The next house we paid cash for some years later was many times more expensive and we had the cash in three weeks. Today, just our television bill is well over $1 million *every* month. How could we borrow enough money each month to pay for that? Thank God, borrowed money is not our source—HE IS!

You cannot receive these things just because I tell you about them. You have to take the scriptures on prosperity and meditate on them until they become a reality in your heart, until you know prosperity belongs to you. Once you have a revelation of divine prosperity in your spirit, you won't allow Satan to take it from you. *The Word of God is the source of your prosperity.* The Word is the source of everything you need in life. *Faith comes by hearing, and hearing by the Word of God.* Don't look to people to meet your needs. Look to the Word. Satan will try to convince you that you can never walk in prosperity, but don't look at the circumstances around you. Look at the Word that says it is yours.

There are different areas of poverty just as there are different areas of sickness. A headache is one thing; terminal cancer is another. I wouldn't enjoy either of them. In the same way, you can have lack in some areas or you can have total lack: You can be without food to eat or without quite enough to make ends meet. Again. I wouldn't enjoy either one.

Why should I? Why should I settle for only a part of the blessing of Abraham? The Word says I am entitled to all the blessing of Abraham.

Don't just believe God to meet your needs. Believe Him for a surplus of prosperity so that you can help others. We here in America are a blessed people financially. We have been called to finance the gospel to the world. According to 2 Corinthians 9:8, AMPC, we should be "self-sufficient [possessing enough to require no aid or support and furnished in abundance for every good work and charitable donation]. Verse 11 says, Thus you will be enriched in all things and in every way, so that you can be generous...." Isn't that better than just barely getting by?

If you are furnished in abundance, then you will be able to reach out to others. You will live in a surplus of prosperity. *You will walk in divine prosperity.*

THE
HUNDREDFOLD
RETURN

A nd Jesus answered and said, Verily I say unto you, There is no man that hath left house, or brethren, or sisters, or father, or mother, or wife, or children, or lands, for my sake, and the gospel's, but he shall receive an hundredfold now in this time, houses, and brethren, and sisters, and mothers, and children, and lands, with persecutions; and in the world to come eternal life" (Mark 10:29-30).

Some years ago a new awareness of the hundredfold return began to grow in my spirit and mind. The Lord began to speak to me about just how great the hundred-fold return is. He wanted me to meditate on it and let it become a powerful reality in my spirit. Revelation knowledge of God's Word grows in you like the seed planted in Mark 4:26-29. A man scatters seed in the ground. He rises and sleeps night and day while the seed sprouts and grows and increases—he knows not how. When allowed to grow, there comes a day when the grain is ripe and the harvest is ready.

The Word of God works like that. The Word is the seed. If it is planted in the heart and watered and allowed to

> "AND THESE ARE THEY WHICH ARE SOWN ON GOOD GROUND; SUCH AS HEAR THE WORD, AND RECEIVE IT, AND BRING FORTH FRUIT, SOME THIRTYFOLD, SOME SIXTY AND SOME AN HUNDRED."
>
> Mark 4:20

grow and increase, it will come to maturity and produce the harvest of results. "And these are they which are sown on good ground; such as hear the word, and receive it, and bring forth fruit, some thirtyfold, some sixty, and some an hundred" (Mark 4:20).

The Word will produce according to how *you* hear it, how *you* receive it, and how *you* bring forth fruit. These returns are brought forth by believing and acting on God's Word and by the confession of your mouth. Some hearers will bring forth no fruit because they will allow other things to choke the Word (Mark 4:19). Some will bring forth fruit. Some will bring forth a thirtyfold return, some will bring forth a sixtyfold return, and some will bring forth one hundredfold.

As we study the hundredfold return, allow this Word to grow in you. Meditate in it and think about what the Word is saying to you. I will share it with you just as the Lord shared it with me over a period of months.

The first thing the Lord led me to realize was just how great the hundredfold return really is. You give $1 for the gospel's sake and the full hundredfold return would be $100. Ten dollars would be $1,000. A hundredfold return on $1,000 would be $100,000.

Webster's New 20th Century Dictionary says that *hundredfold* means "one hundred times the bulk or measure of anything."

Mark 10:30 is a very good deal. Where in the natural world are you offered the return of 100 times your investment? In the natural world if you double your money, you do well. If you receive 10 times your investment, it is a marvelous deal, but who even talks in terms of 100 times an investment.

After I let what the Word offers us in the hundredfold return become a reality to me, the Lord led me to continually give thanks for the hundredfold return. Whenever I thought about it, I would say, "Thank You, Father, for the hundredfold return offered in Your Word. It is such a generous return, and it belongs to me." I would say any faith words of praise that came into my spirit in regard to continually thanking God for the hundredfold return. This thanksgiving kept my faith active and operative to receive. Continually confessing the hundredfold return causes the seed of Mark 10:30 to grow.

For years Kenneth and I have acted on Mark 10:30 in our giving and believed for the hundredfold return. When we receive offerings into this ministry, we believe for the hundredfold return to come back to those who give. Many of you have received letters from us thanking you for your gift and believing with you for the hundredfold return. As we write the letter to be sent to those who stand with us in this ministry financially, we pray and believe for whatever we write in the letter. We expect it to come to pass. Mark 10:30 has been vital to us for a long time. But recently, it seems that not only has the seed sprouted, but the blade, the ear, and the full grain in the ear have

ripened within our spirits. AND WE HAVE BEEN
HARVESTING A CROP!

I am believing that what I am sharing with you will be
as great a blessing to you as it has been to us. I want you
to enjoy the harvest of the hundredfold return in a greater
measure than ever before in your own life.

Months and months after the Lord instructed me to
continually give thanks for the hundredfold return, Kenneth
and I were in Hawaii for a convention. We had some days
before the meeting to relax and enjoy ourselves. One day
as we were discussing the Word, we got on the subject of
the hundredfold return. Kenneth said, "Well, you know,
we never have received the *full* hundredfold return on
our giving."

I thought about it. No, the full hundredfold return
had never been manifested in our lives, even though great
returns have come back on us. Even then the hundredfold
return on our giving, both personally and through our
ministry, would be millions of dollars. Yet, if the Word
said it, and it does, then we know that it belongs to us.
These thoughts went through my mind, and I said, "Well,
we aren't through yet," and he agreed. We could have
stopped further revelation right then by saying, "I guess
we have tenfold faith" or by giving in to what we could
see. There is one thing about the Copelands that most
of you have heard: *We play till we win!* One secret I will
share with you about living by faith is KEEP PLAYING!
THE GAME ISN'T OVER YET!

During the next few days that conversation stayed on
my mind. I thought about it from time to time. You know,
that is what meditation is: to dwell or fix your mind on
something. During the convention just as a challenge

to my faith—as though to declare that the Word is true and I *will* receive the full hundredfold return in Jesus' Name—I said, "All right, as a challenge to my faith, I am going to put $10 into the offering and believe for an immediate return of $1,000 to pay some of the expenses of our trip." Deliberately, I gave according to Mark 10:30 and believed for the full hundredfold return. I made the decision to receive—and to receive immediately.

The next day I spoke at the ladies' luncheon. A woman that I did not know came to the table. She said that she and her husband were at the hotel for a vacation and did not know that we were going to be there. She handed me a check and said that they were supporters of our ministry and gave on a regular basis, but this check was for Kenneth and me personally. IT WAS A CHECK FOR $500. Nobody had ever handed me a check for $500 at a ladies' luncheon before! There was 50 percent of my return by the next day (not 50 percent of my gift, but 50 percent of my return!). I was so thrilled because I knew it was a direct response to my believing for the hundredfold return on the $10 I gave the previous afternoon. Praise the Lord!

Throughout the remainder of the meeting, I continued to meditate on the hundredfold return and continually thanked God for it. The last night of the convention during the offering, someone read Mark 10:29-30. As he read that scripture aloud, the answer I had been looking for jumped out at me, "BUT HE SHALL RECEIVE AN HUNDREDFOLD NOW IN THIS TIME". I heard it as "NOW IN THIS LIFE." I checked and found that several translations say "in this life" or "in this present life." *W.E. Vine's Expository Dictionary of New Testament Words* says, "In this lifetime."

Jesus said whatever you release or give up for His sake and the gospel's you will receive a hundred times as much now in this life. He did not say it would come in two weeks, but He said it would come in this life. Glory to God! Here was the answer. I had given $10, believing for the hundredfold return. Fifty percent of that return came to me within 24 hours—that meant $500 was still out there coming to me in this life. I realized that the hundredfold return is continually working, coming to me as long as I keep my faith active in its behalf.

None of the blessings of God work automatically, even though they belong to us. They become manifested in our lives as we exercise our faith to receive them. Healing belongs to every believer, but that great blessing is enjoyed only by those who exercise their faith to receive it. Tithing carries great benefits and rewards, but if you don't tithe according to the Word and use your faith to receive those benefits, they are not manifested in your life as they should be. In the same way the hundredfold return is a powerful force in the believer's financial blessing, but you have to release your faith to receive all that the Word offers you. The force of faith must be applied by the Word of God in your heart and by the confession of your mouth.

In this life was the answer to our conversation a few days before about the full hundredfold not being manifested. We knew we were abundantly blessed financially, that we had operated in divine prosperity, and that whatever we desired in the material realm we had asked for and received. We knew we had already received large returns on our giving. When God revealed to me that ALL of the hundredfold return of ALL that we had given was out there coming to us and that it would come to us *in this life*, I could see that if we would exercise our faith before we leave this life, ALL that return would come and had been continually coming to us all along.

UPDATE: Since 1977 when the book was written, our ministry income (for 1990) has increased 818 percent. Our hundredfold return is working!

In the past we had used our faith where Mark 10:29-30 was concerned; but now I can see that although we did not negate our confession for the hundredfold return, we did after a period of time allow the determination of faith to wane. By then, we would be believing for the hundredfold on more recent offerings. We would receive a partial return but fail to stand fast for the full return on our past giving, and after a while we would forget. It was still out there. It was still ours but without the pressure of our faith, it could stop.

I shared this from the Word with Jerry and Carolyn Savelle weeks later. Jerry told me that when they were first learning to give, he would stand for the hundredfold return *until* it came. He was in a position financially where he had to have the full return just to get by. Consequently, he believed it in. I shared with them that the full hundredfold return will come in if we keep our faith active and operating for it. They received the Word and began to expect. The next day a woman brought a $500 check by the office for Carolyn. Carolyn had given and was believing God for the money to landscape their new home. Her faith activated the return to come to her.

The hundredfold return on all our giving already belonged to us, but lack of diligence (failure to continually confess the Word and release faith for the hundredfold return) permitted the return to lie fallow in *Accounts*

Receivable. *Accounts Receivable* is money that belongs to a company, but sometimes collecting it is another matter. *We have learned how to collect!* What we have learned recently about the hundredfold return is the way to continually keep that hundredfold engaged and operating in our behalf. Now we can continually release our faith for *all* of the hundredfold return on *all* our giving. (Since this great return already belongs to you and is just waiting for you to apply faith pressure, you can receive the hundredfold on your past giving as well. *The hundredfold is retroactive.* Praise the Lord!)

Now think this through with me the way I did as I began to see into it. Kenneth and I had been living by faith for 20 years. We had been giving and believing for the return on our giving. In those 20 years we had been abundantly blessed. God has blessed us with whatever we have desired from Him. In 1968 when we first heard about how to walk in faith, our income was $3,594.37, below poverty level, and we were not on welfare! Since we have been living on the Word, we have increased and been blessed with every material blessing. The more we give, the more we receive. The more we receive, the more we give and the larger our hundredfold return becomes. What will it be like after we have lived this way another 20 years, and then another? Glory to God! Our second 20 years will be better than our first 20 years, and the first 20 years have been beyond what the natural mind could believe! Just think what it will be like by the time I am 100 years old and Kenneth is 105!

I can see how the Body of Christ is going to end up with all the money! No matter how much the amount of your giving increases, you are still offered the hundredfold return, and it is still guaranteed to come to you in this life!

That night in Hawaii as I began to see into these things, I got so excited. We were up late visiting with friends, and I did not have a chance to share with Ken what I had received about the hundredfold return. It was still coming together piece by piece.

God Is Faithful to Perform His Word

Now I want to share in detail a testimony of how God is faithful to perform His Word in our behalf. The convention was over and we planned to leave for the airport at 10:30 the next morning. Instead of waking up at 7 a.m. as planned, I got up at 8:30 a.m. Though I didn't expect to have time for breakfast, things worked out that way. I went downstairs ahead of the family to get a table. I decided to eat inside instead of on the terrace because of time. When it was my turn, a man stepped in front of me and got the table that should have been mine. The coffee shop was full, so I waited. Then I followed the hostess all the way to the back and around the corner (the room is L-shaped). You can't even see this area from most of the restaurant. There was an empty table for four. I do not recall seeing another empty table. I started to sit at one side of the table but decided to move to the other side so I could watch for Ken. I was not following the voice of the Lord. I was following my own spirit without really thinking about it, and I was just flowing with what came next.

In a few minutes a lady came to the table. I had met her only for a moment the day of the luncheon. She said as she took a ring from her finger, "God told me to give you this." I didn't look at the ring but only at the woman.

She seemed upset, and I thought that she was doing something that she did not really want to do.

I said, "Why don't you pray about it a little longer? I wouldn't want you to regret it later."

She said, "Oh no, It isn't that. I have just never had anything like this happen to me before. I have been impressed for several days to give you this ring, but I didn't know for sure that it was the Lord. Last night while Ken was speaking it got stronger, so I prayed, 'Lord, if You want me to give Gloria Copeland this ring, have her sit next to me at breakfast in the morning.' "

We usually don't even come down for breakfast! In that big, crowded coffee shop, I had been seated right next to her table. I even got up and moved to the other side, sitting as close as I could possibly get without sitting at her table! I had no idea that God had a wonderful blessing waiting for me that morning at breakfast, but the hundredfold return was working for me in a beautiful way.

I picked up the ring and looked at it. It is one of the most unusual rings I have ever seen—two squares of emeralds and diamonds set in gold. The two squares rotate as my hand moves. It is a stunning piece of jewelry. I received this beautiful ring from the lady in faith, knowing that God would not have instructed her to give such a treasure unless He had something great in store for her. You have to give in faith, but it is also important to receive in faith.

Then I remembered the hundredfold return. The last time we were in Hawaii in the same hotel, I had been impressed to give a diamond ring to someone the morning we were getting ready to come home. I gave it, and she told me later that it was just like the one she had seen in a window years ago and was just what she wanted. When I gave it, I believed for the hundredfold return to come to me. The beautiful ring that I had just received was a direct return on the one I had given away. I had wanted a pinkie ring, and this is the most beautiful one I have ever seen. When I put it on, it fit perfectly. I was jumping up and down on the inside! I knew that what I had just received from the Word of God in the last few days had caused this blessing to come to me. The return was mine all along, but my faith had been energized to receive without delay! The hundredfold return was working for me. Thank God for the wonderful hundredfold return! Even though the ring I received was much finer than the one I gave, much of my hundredfold is still out there working—coming to me. How exciting.

I still had not shared with Ken the great and powerful revelation I had received—one that has continued to grow and expand ever since. When we got on the airplane, the first thing I did was tell him what I had seen in the Word. He got excited too. As I reminded him of the ring I had given away, I looked down at the beautiful ring I was now enjoying. It moves constantly, the two squares going around. I said, "Look! That's my hundredfold return ring. I received it as a return, and just like my hundredfold return, it is continually moving—working. The hundred-fold return is continually working in our behalf, coming to us in this life."

I give testimony to the glory of God just as any other believer would. We have continued to meditate on the hundredfold return. We have read the scriptures and thought about them. We continually thank God for our return and confess that the full hundredfold is working, coming to us. We confess that we are receiving the full hundredfold return of all we have given for Jesus' sake, or the gospel's. Kenneth and I are still saying these things with our mouths, and we are still receiving. We have kept our faith active. We become more and more thrilled as we share with others what we have learned. The seed of Mark 10:29-30 has begun harvesting a greater crop than ever before in our lives. Glory to God! Harvest time is here.

Our hundredfold return is working and coming to us. One unusual thing that happened as a direct result of our faith came, totally unexpected, from an organization I had spoken for. When they invited me to speak, they said that they would not give me an honorarium. It was the only place I had ever been invited to speak that did not even offer gasoline money, but I had been told in advance, so I was not surprised. We had a great meeting, and I forgot about it. When I returned from Hawaii, there was a check for $150 from this organization with a note saying they were terribly sorry to be so late in sending the honorarium. We had never received an honorarium a year late! The hundredfold return is working, coming to us—and from the most unexpected sources. God's hundredfold return is working miraculously in our lives.

What I have been sharing with you sounds like science fiction to some people, but there are thousands of believers who are believing God financially, who dare to stand on God's Word where prosperity is concerned. This will mean more to those of you who have already been believing God and using your faith in the financial area. Start believing God on the level where you can believe. Study Kenneth's book *The Laws of Prosperity* until you know from God's Word that it is His will for you to prosper. You will soon find that when you are ready to believe you receive the hundredfold return. Dare to believe what the Word says. You are a believer. You can believe.

I shared these scriptures about the hundredfold return with a man on our staff. He had just given away a piece of equipment worth several thousand dollars and was believing for a tenfold return because he knew from past experiences that he could believe in tenfold, but a hundredfold return seemed a little shaky. I was so thrilled to share what the Lord had given me concerning the hundredfold return because I knew that once the Word had been revealed to him, he would be able to obtain his full hundredfold return. "Faith cometh by hearing and hearing by the Word of God." After he saw further into the hundredfold return and that it belonged to him, he no longer hesitated to step out and believe for it. It no longer seemed beyond his reach.

There are thousands of people who are Partners with this ministry. I am believing that you can take what I have shared with you and plant the seed of Mark 10:29-30. I am believing that you will meditate on this scripture and allow it to grow in you until you harvest the hundredfold return on all of your giving! "And He said to them, Is the lamp brought in to be put under a peck measure or under a bed, and not [to be put] on the lampstand? [Things are hidden temporarily only as a means to revelation.] For there is nothing hidden except to be revealed, nor is anything [temporarily] kept secret except in order that it may be made known. If any man has ears to hear, let him be listening and let him perceive and comprehend. And He said to them, Be careful what you are hearing. The measure [of thought and study] you give [to the truth you hear] will be the measure [of virtue and knowledge] that comes back to you—and more [besides] will be given to you who hear. For to him who has will more be given; and from him who has nothing, even what he has will be taken away [by force]" (Mark 4:21-25, AMPC).

The truth won't work for you just because it works for me. The Word will work for *you* when it becomes a reality in *your* heart. It is working in my life because I have meditated on it and allowed it to become a reality to me. I have received and acted accordingly. The Word says that the measure of thought and study you give to the truth you hear will be the measure of virtue and knowledge that comes back to you. Jesus said, "Be careful how you hear." The more you think about the Word of God and confess it with your mouth, the faster that seed will grow within you—first the blade, then the ear, then the full grain in the ear. Then harvest time is here! The respect, reverence and value you place on the Word you hear determines the power (virtue) that operates on your behalf.

Some of the things that stop the Word of God from producing its full capabilities are listed in Mark 4. These things steal from you not only in finances but in every area of life.

1. Satan comes to talk you out of it.
2. The Word doesn't root in your heart, and when trouble or persecution comes, you become offended and believe circumstances rather than what the Word says.
3. Cares and anxieties of the world.
4. Distractions of the age.
5. Pleasure and delight and false glamour.

6. Deceitfulness of riches.

7. Craving and passionate desire for other things creep in and choke and suffocate the Word. Then the Word becomes fruitless.

(These are taken from the *Amplified Bible, Classic Edition.*)

The ones who received are talked about in Mark 4:20 (AMPC):

"And those sown on the good (well-adapted) soil are the ones who hear the Word and receive and accept and welcome it and bear fruit—some thirty times as much as was sown, some sixty times as much, and some [even] a hundred times as much."

Some in Mark 4 didn't let the Word bear any fruit. Others let different things stop the Word from working faith in their hearts. Some did receive thirty times as much as was sown. Which is, by the way, a great return. Others received sixtyfold. Some one hundredfold.

Sowing and reaping is not a doctrine. It is a spiritual law or principle. It works in anything, not just money or material things. You sow love, you receive back love. Sow hate and discord and that will be returned to you multiplied.

Some don't agree that there is a hundredfold return or that this scripture in Mark 10:29-30 applies to money. Because of the way the Lord gave it to me and because of other scriptures, I believe the hundredfold return is available. There are many things involved. I don't think most people will receive it because it is not automatic, but I believe it is available to every believer. I personally am believing God for His best.

What if you were to believe for the hundredfold return and only actually receive the thirtyfold return. Is that not better than receiving no return because you did not attempt to receive by faith?

If this is too hard for you now, then when you give, act on Luke 6:38:

"Give, and [gifts] will be given to you; good measure, pressed down, shaken together, and running over, will they pour into [the pouch formed by] the bosom [of your robe and used as a bag]. For with the measure you deal out [with the measure you use when you confer benefits on others], it will be measured back to you" (AMPC).

This says what you give will be pressed down, shaken together, and running over. That is definitely a great increase. Sounds like a hundredfold return!

Galatians 6:7 is in the context of talking about giving. The Word says, "Be not deceived; God is not mocked: for whatsoever a man soweth, that shall he also reap." Then in verse 9, "And let us not be weary in well doing: for in due season we shall reap, if we faint not."

Remember, Mark 10:30 says, "With persecutions." In the financial area return comes with persecution (or opposition). We must not faint but believe God. Refuse to allow the devil to steal the full hundredfold return that is available to you.

Today, the hundredfold return is not the reason we give. We give out of obedience to God. We give because we love God. We give because we love people. It is not to be our motive for giving. It is a benefit of giving—a principle of blessing from God our Father.

Prophecy

I believe that the following prophecy concerning finances and the hundredfold return will be a blessing to you. The Lord spoke these words through Charles Capps in Honolulu, Hawaii, February 1, 1978. (Note: *Inversion* means "a turning upside down or inside out; reversal of position.")

Financial inversion shall increase in these days. For you see, it is My desire to move in the realm of your financial prosperity. But release Me, saith the Lord, release Me that I may come in your behalf and move on your behalf.

For yes, yes, yes, there shall be in this hour financial distress here and there. The economy shall go up and it will go down; but those that learn to walk in the Word, they shall see the PROSPERITY OF THE WORD come forth in this hour in a way that has not been seen by men in days past.

Yes, there's coming a FINANCIAL INVERSION in the world's system. It's been held in reservoirs of wicked men for days on end. But the end is nigh. Those reservoirs shall be tapped and shall be drained into the gospel of Jesus Christ. It shall be done, saith the Lord. It shall be done IN THE TIME ALLOTTED and so shall it be that the Word of the Lord shall come to pass that the wealth of the sinner is laid up for the just.

Predominantly in two ways shall it be done in this hour. Those that have hoarded up and stored because of the inspiration of the evil one and held the money from the gospel shall be converted and drawn into the kingdom and then shall it release that reservoir into the kingdom. But many, many will not. They'll not heed the voice of the Word of God. They'll turn aside to this and they'll turn to that and they'll walk in their own ways, but their ways will not work in this hour. It'll dwindle and it'll slip away as though it were in bags with holes in them. It'll go here and it'll go there and they'll wonder why it's not working now. "It worked in days past," they'll say.

But it shall be, saith the Lord, that THE WORD OF THE LORD SHALL RISE WITHIN MEN— men of God of low esteem in the financial world— that shall claim the Word of God to be their very own and walk in the light of it as it has been set forth in the Word and give. They'll begin to give small at first because that's all they have, but then it will increase, and THROUGH THE HUNDRED- FOLD RETURN, so shall it be that the reservoirs that have held the riches in days past, so shall it return to the hands of the giver. BECAUSE OF THE HUNDREDFOLD RETURN SHALL THE RESERVOIRS BE LOST FROM THE WICKED AND TURNED TO THE GOSPEL. For it shall be, it shall be in this hour that you will see things that you've never dreamed come to pass. Oh, it'll be strong at first in ways, then it will grow greater and greater until men will be astounded and the world will stand in awe because the ways of men have failed and the ways of God shall come forth.

As men walk in My Word, so shall they walk in the ways of the Lord. Oh yes, there will be some who say, "Yes, but God's ways are higher, surely higher than our ways, and we can't walk in those." It's true that the ways of God are higher. They are higher than your ways as the heavens are above the earth, but I'll teach you to walk in My ways. I never did say you couldn't walk in My ways. Now learn to walk in it. Learn to give. So shall the inversion of the financial system revert and so shall it be that the gospel of the kingdom shall be preached to all the world, and THERE SHALL BE NO LACK IN THE KINGDOM. Those that give shall walk in the ways of the supernatural! They shall be known abroad. MY WORD SHALL SPREAD AND THE KNOWLEDGE OF THE LORD SHALL FILL ALL THE EARTH IN THE DAY AND THE HOUR IN WHICH YE STAND. Ye shall see it and know it, for it is of Me, and it shall come to pass, saith the Lord.

HOW TO RECEIVE FROM GOD

G od does not will one thing and say another. It would be dishonest and unjust for Him not to reveal His will to you and then hold you responsible for walking uprightly before Him.

Paul's Spirit-directed prayer for the Church is "that ye might be filled with the knowledge of his will in all wisdom and spiritual understanding" (Colossians 1:9).

God's Word is His will. His Word is supernatural and it is alive! The Holy Spirit is sent to reveal this supernatural Word to you. He makes the instruction of the Father a reality. Read the Bible with the knowledge that God had it written for your benefit—not for His. He is already quite successful!

The Word is God speaking to you, teaching you how to live an abundant and successful life.

> "IF YE ABIDE IN ME, AND MY WORDS ABIDE IN YOU, YE SHALL ASK WHAT YE WILL, AND IT SHALL BE DONE UNTO YOU."
>
> John 15:7

Jesus said, "If ye abide in me, and my words abide in you, ye shall ask what ye will, and it shall be done unto you" (John 15:7).

God's Word in you is the key to answered prayer.

Your Father wants you to be victorious in this life and enjoy all the rights and privileges that Jesus purchased for you. He desires that you keep His Word because it will keep you whole—spirit, soul and body.

The world should see a Christian as the Word sees him—a man able to control his circumstances with every physical, mental and spiritual need met.

The Bible tells you who you are and what you can do in Christ. As a born-again believer, you are in Christ. You are a member of the Body of Christ.

The Bible is not a book to be admired and given a place of honor in the bookshelf. It is your Reference Book on living. Your very life depends on what you find in it. It is the "how to" of everyday life. Keep it with you.

The Bible is God's wisdom made available to man and written in man's words. Read it positively, not as a set of rules but as the open door to freedom. "And ye shall know the truth, and the truth shall make you free" (John 8:32).

The truth makes you free! It does not put you in bondage.

God's Formula for Success

"This Book of the Law shall not depart out of your mouth, but you shall meditate on it day and night, that you may observe and do according to all that is written in it. For then you shall make your way prosperous, and then you shall deal wisely and have good success" (Joshua 1:8, AMPC).

God's success formula begins with keeping His Word in your mouth. *Talk God's Word.*

God gave Israel these instructions: "And these words, which I command thee this day, shall be in thine heart: And thou shalt teach them diligently unto thy children, and shalt talk of them when thou sittest in thine house, and when thou walkest by the way, and when thou liest down, and when thou risest up" (Deuteronomy 6:6-7).

God told Israel to talk His Word when they sat down, when they walked, when they lay down, and when they rose up. That is all the time!

How could that be possible? Jesus said that "out of the abundance of the heart the mouth speaketh" (Matthew 12:34). The words you put in yourself are the words that come out. What words do you see and listen to most of the time—television, radio, newspapers, novels—or God's Word? Listen to yourself talk and you will know what is in you in abundance. If you are talking doubt, fear, sickness and lack, that is what is in you in abundance. Your source of information must be changed!

The stream of things in the world is negative. Unless you take action against the world order *with the Word of God,* your mouth will speak from experience, circumstance and tradition.

Jesus said, "For verily I say unto you, That whosoever shall say unto this mountain, Be thou removed, and be thou cast into the sea; and shall not doubt in his heart, but shall believe that those things which he saith shall come to pass; he shall have whatsoever he saith" (Mark 11:23).

You receive in this life just what you say with your mouth. The Word in your mouth is your faith speaking.

The words you speak are what you believe.

Your words can be for you or against you. They bring you health or sickness. Your words decide whether you live in abundance or lack. Your words give you victory or cause you to be defeated. Solomon, the wisest and richest man of the Old Testament, said, "You are snared by the words of your mouth." You are snared by your words, or you are set free by your words.

For out of the abundance of the heart the mouth speaketh. The mouth speaks according to what you put in your heart. "A good man out of the good treasure of the heart bringeth forth good things" (Matthew 12:35). Put God's Word in your heart, and you will speak God's Word with your mouth. God's Word in your mouth will cause good things to happen in your life.

Meditate in God's Word

You put God's Word in your heart by meditation in His Word. You do not change believing in your heart by just wanting to change it. *You only change how you believe by the Word of God.*

"So then faith cometh by hearing, and hearing by the word of God" (Romans 10:17). The only way faith comes into the heart is by hearing the Word, and the only way faith can be developed is through the Word. There is no shortcut.

Meditation in God's Word is a necessity in God's success formula. Keep His Word before you and meditate. Dwell upon the Word in your thought life day and night. Meditation is more than just reading. Meditation is *fixing your mind on the Word* so that *you do all* that is written therein. You will gain revelation and insight into the Word that you never could gain by only reading.

In meditating in the Word, you are applying that Word to yourself personally. You are allowing the Holy Spirit to make God's Word a reality in your heart.

You are carefully pondering how this Word applies to your life. You are dwelling on how this Word from the Lord changes your situation, or perhaps you simply receive the quiet revelation of *that means me!* You are placing yourself in agreement with what God says about you. You are seeing yourself as He sees you!

As long as God's Word is just a Book—even a Holy Book—you will not act on it. Until the Bible becomes God dealing with you, it will not be active and powerful in your life.

Through meditation the integrity of God's Word becomes a reality to you. As the truth is revealed in your spirit, you will begin to do all that is written in it. Doing God's Word is the end result of keeping God's words in your mouth and meditating on His Word. Only acting on God's Word guarantees success.

One of the greatest enemies of faith is *mental assent.* Mental assent agrees that the Word is true. Mental assent sounds good but enjoys *no results* because it *only agrees* that the Word is true—mental assent does not act on the Word.

Mental assent says, "I believe the Bible is true from Genesis to Revelation." But when it comes to apply that Word *personally,* mental assent then says, "I know the Bible says that by His stripes I am healed, but I feel sick, so I must be sick."

Mental assent does not act from faith in the Word but acts on what it sees and feels. People who just agree that the Word is true do not walk by faith but by sight.

Beware of the trap of mental assent. It is subtle because it sounds good. A good deal of time mental assent can be tagged by the words *but* and *if*. These two little words will rob you of your confession of faith. Replace confessions of doubt with the Word of God.

Acting on the Word

Jesus gives us an example of two men and the way they responded after hearing the Word. The wise man acted on the Word, and the foolish man mentally assented to the Word. You can be either man.

"Therefore whosoever heareth these sayings of mine, and doeth them, I will liken him unto a wise man, which built his house upon a rock: And the rain descended, and the floods came, and the winds blew, and beat upon that house; and it fell not: for it was founded upon a rock. And every one that heareth these sayings of mine, and doeth them not, shall be likened unto a foolish man, which built his house upon the sand: And the rain descended, and the floods came, and the winds blew, and beat upon that house; and it fell: and great was the fall of it" (Matthew 7:24-27).

Knowing what the Word says is not enough. You must act on that knowledge to get results. Both men heard the Word and both houses experienced the storm, but the results were different!

Acting on the Word put a foundation under the wise man's house that could not be moved, and his house suffered no loss.

The foolish man, who heard the Word but did not do it, had no foundation when the floods came. His house may have been easier to build, but it had no power to stand.

Because meditation makes God's Word a reality to you, it shuts the door to mental assent and opens the door wide to doing God's Word. It not only gets your thoughts but also your actions in line with God's will for you. As truths are revealed to you in the Word, apply them to your circumstances and do them. You be the wise man that acts on the Word. When the adversities of life come against your house, it will stand because the foundation of doing God's Word will make it stand.

You will learn to act on the Word of God just as you would the word of your doctor, lawyer, or best friend.*

To put this formula into action, find out what God says in the Word about the need in your life. In His Word, you will find God's answer to every problem common to man. For every evil Satan can throw at mankind, our Father has provided the Word to overcome that evil. Prosperity and good success are yours through God's Word. "If ye abide in me, and my words abide in you, ye shall ask what ye will, and it shall be done unto you" (John 15:7).

To receive from God, you must make your thoughts, actions, and words be in agreement with what God says belongs to you. *You* are the determining factor in receiving from God. God's Word does not change. God's will does not change. If you want to receive from God, YOU must change your believing and saying to agree with Him.

We receive by faith. Well, what is faith? It is so simple, yet many make it seem complex or unattainable. Faith is believing what God says in His Word regardless of what you see with your eyes or hear with your ears or feel with your senses. Faith believes God's Word no matter what the circumstances say. *The Amplified Bible, Classic Edition*

---

in Hebrews 11:1 says that faith is perceiving as real fact what is not yet revealed to the senses.

Faith is trust. If I told you something but offered no proof to back my words, you would have to trust me in order to believe it. If you said, "You will have to show me before I will believe it," you put no confidence in my integrity. When you receive or reject what God says in His Word concerning you, you are dealing with His integrity.

God's Word is good. The Bible says that God is not a man that He should lie (Numbers 23:19).

You may think, "I would never call God Almighty a liar," but that is exactly what you do every time you allow your words and actions to contradict what you know God says about you in His Word. You are acting in fear instead of in faith—fear that God will not perform His Word in your life. What an insult to the Father!

God's success formula has produced in our lives over and over and over again. *It has never failed to produce.* We have personally used this formula to receive healing, airplanes, houses, office buildings, equipment, clothes, cars, boats, wisdom, guidance, help with our children, and national radio and television coverage—to name a few. We have used the Word to receive in every area of our lives. The Bible tells us that the just shall *live* by faith. We have lived by faith and enjoyed tremendous blessings.

When you get ready to release your faith, use whatever scripture the Lord leads you to use. Don't go to God with the problem. Don't pray the problem—pray the answer. Present to God the Word that covers your need and say, "I believe it!"

You Can Have What You Say

Let's go through the faith process from start to finish and find out what it takes on your part to believe God for something you cannot see. Get ready to release your faith right now for whatever you need from God. Mark 11: 22-24, will work for any need. "And Jesus answering saith unto them, Have faith in God. For verily I say unto you, That whosoever shall say unto this mountain, Be thou removed, and be thou cast into the sea; and shall not doubt in his heart, but shall believe that those things which he saith shall come to pass; he shall have whatsoever he saith. Therefore I say unto you, What things soever ye desire, when ye pray, believe that ye receive them, and ye shall have them."

"Whosoever shall say unto this mountain." According to Jesus, in order to change things *you are to speak to the mountain*. The mountain is the obstacle or need in your life. Let's assume that your need is financial—you just simply need more money to live and to give. Say this: "Poverty, I speak to you in the Name of Jesus, and I command you to be removed from my presence and my life. I will no longer tolerate you. I forbid you to operate against me in any way."

You do not talk to God about the problem. Talk to Him about the answer—the Word of God. You speak to the mountain and tell it what to do. Jesus spoke to the wind and water and said, "Peace, be still!" He spoke to the fig tree and said, "No man eat fruit of thee hereafter forever." Guess what? Nobody did! Most people want God to talk to the mountain for them, but HE WILL NOT. He has given the believer that authority; and if you want results, do it His way. TALK TO THE MOUNTAIN!

When God delegates authority, He delegates authority! Adam proved that in the Garden when he committed high treason. God knew what was going on in the Garden when Adam was being tempted. Even though the consequences were so hideous, God would not repudiate the authority He had given Adam. "And God said, Let us make man in our image, after our likeness: and let them have dominion over the fish of the sea, and over the fowl of the air, and over the cattle, and over all the earth, and over every creeping thing that creepeth upon the earth" (Genesis 1:26). "But of the tree of the knowledge of good and evil, thou shalt not eat of it: for in the day that thou eatest thereof thou shalt surely die" (Genesis 2:17). God's Word was all Adam needed to make him successful. Satan as a serpent was a creature, and Adam had authority over all living creatures. He should have used his authority and commanded Satan to flee and never come back. God had given Adam instruction not to eat of the tree of the knowledge of good and evil. Adam had God's Word and he had dominion. God would not override Adam's authority.

There is another side to that story: God is not going to override your authority either. He has given you authority in the earth. He has given you instructions in His Word to put you over in every situation. He will let you die sick if you choose to do so. You would have to ignore every healing scripture in the Bible and all that Jesus bought for you when He bore your sicknesses and carried your diseases, but you have the authority to go ahead and die. God will not stop you. On the other hand, you have the authority to take His Word and command your body to be healed in the Name of Jesus. "So be subject to God. Resist the devil [stand firm against him], and he will flee from you" (James 4:7, AMPC).

Some religious men today, who advocate that believers should welcome suffering, teach that God is allowing the loss of your business, your health, or some other curse in order to teach you something. Therefore, if God is allowing it, you have no defense against it. You are just supposed to brace up and suffer "like a good little trooper." If you believe this teaching, you automatically put yourself in position for Satan to whip you and whip you badly. This is directly opposed to the operation of faith and your God-given authority. It is contrary to God's Word that says, "Let no man say when he is tempted, I am tempted of God: for God cannot be tempted with evil, neither tempteth he any man.... Do not err, my beloved brethren. Every good gift and every perfect gift is from above, and cometh down from the Father of lights, with whom is no variableness, neither shadow of turning" (James 1:13, 16-17).

How can you resist if you think God is blessing you with cancer? That sounds so blasphemous that it is hard for me to say. Yet that is just what some would have you believe. *Satan and God have not changed places.* Satan is not making believers rich while God makes them sick. When you examine it with your religious head turned off, it is not hard to figure out where this error originated. Religious error trains you to enforce your own defeat. Every believer who embraces suffering certainly makes Satan's job to kill, steal and destroy much easier. You are told in God's Word to believe that God is the rewarder, not the destroyer. "For whoever would come near to God must [necessarily] believe that God exists and that He is the rewarder of those who earnestly and diligently seek Him [out]" (Hebrews 11:6, AMPC).

This error does, however, have an element of truth in it. GOD IS ALLOWING WHATEVER YOU ALLOW! He has given you authority, and according to His Word, *you* can have what *you* say. He will allow you to be sick, lost in sin, and bound in poverty. God will allow you to die before your time. It is not His will for you, but He remains true to His Word. "If we are faithless...He remains true (faithful to His Word...), for He cannot deny Himself" (2 Timothy 2:13, AMPC). If you take your God-given authority in the earth and use it against yourself, God will allow it. Adam proved that.

Don't feed on error. Don't feed on anything that robs you of your faith—that creates doubt, fear, defeat, discouragement or distrust. If there is one false teaching in the Church that can defeat you permanently, it is that God is making you suffer in order to teach you. *It will get you killed.* Do you understand that? *It will get you killed!* And what an insult to God who has gone to such lengths to make you free! Isaiah, by the inspiration of the Holy Spirit, says that Jesus bore *your* sicknesses and carried *your* diseases. For God to turn around and put them on you would be a miscarriage of justice. The sacrifice of Jesus was not in vain. He suffered for you and for me, so we would not have to suffer. We are to enter into His suffering (Philippians 3:10). We are to receive what He bore for us and go free from sin, sickness, demons and fear (Galatians 3:13).

"And shall not doubt in his heart." At this point you should have already built the Word into your spirit and taken the time to meditate in God's Word until His Word carries more authority in your life than Satan, circumstances and people. Doubt is eradicated from your heart by time spent hearing and meditating on God's Word. This is not doubt of the head but of the heart. Doubt in the heart (the spirit) is not so much an action taken now as the condition of the heart (the spirit). Doubts in the head are dealt with individually as they attack the mind.

You will have to fulfill the second step in God's success formula—meditating in the Word day and night—in order to successfully operate in faith. We will consider that you have done that and are daily continuing to meditate in the Word. (If this is new to you, get started immediately.) You must continually keep your spirit above all that you guard because out of it flow the forces of life (Proverbs 4:23). If you want what you say to come to pass to your advantage, KEEP YOUR HEART FULL OF THE WORD OF GOD. God's Word is His part of our prayer life. We have His answer to our need right here in the written Word. There is no problem in the universe that can stand against God's Word. He tells us what to do in the spiritual world in order to change the physical world. God's Word is law in the spiritual world and in the physical world. The physical, material world is the servant of the more powerful world of the spirit.

Faith is released in both worlds by words. Words are the bridge between the physical world and the spiritual world. Jesus said, "The words that I speak unto you, they are spirit, and they are life." Jesus spoke from a physical body, but His words were spirit. God's words are the bridge between God and man. Man's words are the bridge between man and God. Both worlds operate on words. Think about that. Anything you get ready to do, you say first. You don't even go to the store without saying it if there is anyone else around. It may surprise you, but neither do you get results in the spiritual world without speaking words. When God created the earth, *He said*. The Holy Spirit was moving (hovering) over the face of the deep. What was He doing? He was waiting—waiting on WORDS. The Holy Spirit did nothing until God spoke. God called His will into substance by speaking words of faith. His words brought the material world into being. "Through faith we understand that the worlds were framed by the word of God, so that things which are seen were not made of things which do appear" (Hebrews 11:3).

Even in the natural world you have to speak the result you want. If I wanted to build a round building but told my builder that I wanted a square one, what do you think I would get? Even though the desire of my heart might be to have a perfectly round building, I WOULD GET WHAT I SAID. So it is in believing God: What you say with your mouth is what you are going to get—even though you might desire something else. If you speak the desired results in prayer but speak contrary to that the rest of the time, you will receive what you continue to say. You are a new creature with authority 24 hours a day. You are the voice of God in the earth. Your voice carries authority in both worlds. God has delegated authority here to you. Your words have authority to create every time you speak, not just when you pray. If you speak positive results in prayer and negative results the rest of the time, your negative words will prevail.

Charles Capps said that the Lord told him this: *I have told My people that they can have what they say, and they are saying what they have.* Saying what you have has no power to change things.

THE KEY TO RECEIVING THE DESIRES OF YOUR HEART IS TO MAKE THE WORDS OF YOUR MOUTH AGREE WITH WHAT YOU WANT!

You not only *can* have what you say, but you *do* have what you say. The Lord spoke these words to me concerning Mark 11:23: *In consistency lies the power.* This verse says a man believes that "those things which he saith" shall come to pass. You are to believe that every word you speak will come to pass, not just the petition you are praying about. If you want your faith to work at the highest level, order your words aright. Make everything you say be in agreement with what God says. Be consistent in saying *only* faith words.

When we learned that we were receiving exactly what we said with our mouths, we got busy and made a quality decision to *say only what we wanted to come to pass.* That sounds simple and it is. The things of God are not difficult to understand, but they are peculiar to the way natural man operates. We had been trained all our lives to operate in man's ways, but through the Word, we began to learn God's higher ways. We were determined students. We made the commitment to speak *only* the words that we wanted to come to pass. Negative talk had to go. Doubt, fear, lack, bondage and sickness were not what we wanted to come to pass, so those words ceased to come out our mouths.

IN CONSISTENCY LIES THE POWER! Make every word that you say work for you. You can change your very existence by making the words of your mouth speak what God says about you. Make a decision that those things which *you* say come to pass. MY EVERY WORD

IS COMING TO PASS. You will have to watch what you say carefully for a while, but if you are diligent, it will become just as hard for you to speak negatively as it now is for you to constantly speak right words.

Husbands and wives, help each other to train your words. When your husband corrects you and says, "That's a bad confession," don't get aggravated.

Just say, "You are right. In the Name of Jesus, I rebuke that bad confession, and I render it powerless to come to pass!" We have to help each other.

"He shall have whatsoever he saith." *Believe your words are coming to pass—not just special words at prayer time, but every word that you speak. Make a decision to speak faith-filled words.*

"Therefore I say unto you, What things soever ye desire, when ye pray, believe that ye receive them, and ye shall have them." If you have already made the decision that every word you say is coming to pass, then you have already fulfilled this step. You spoke to the mountain and told it to be removed from your life. Believe that your words are coming to pass.

Speak whatever you desire to come to pass in the Name of Jesus. Take authority over the money you need and command it to come to you. Whatever you say will come to pass. "Believe that ye receive them and ye shall have them." (You do not have authority over the property of others unless they are offering it for sale. You do not have authority over the will of others.)

If you need healing, speak to your body. Command it to be healed in the Name of Jesus. Command it to function properly. Speak the result you want.

Remember, the key to receiving the desires of your heart is to make the words of your mouth agree with what you want.

You have exercised your faith in God. You have spoken to the obstacle in your way and commanded it to be removed. You have said what you want to come to pass. You believe in the words of your mouth and that what you say will come to pass. You believe that you have received the things you desired when you prayed. Do not waver your words, and YOU SHALL HAVE THEM.

These verses in Mark are the classic faith verses. You may use another scripture that will give you the results you need, but you will still have to make your words continually speak what you desire in order to get those results and you will have to believe that you have received what you prayed. These verses describe the operation of faith. Faith does not operate any other way. To receive from God, follow these instructions.

Nothing Wavering

Once you have prayed, acted on God's Word, and believed that you have received the answer, demand that your actions, thoughts and words agree with what you *have* received. Act as though you have it. Satan knows that unless he can get you to change your confession of faith, his hold over you is broken. *If Satan had any authority of his own, he would not have to depend on deception.* Satan has to trick you into saying what he wants to come to pass. Did you know that Satan can only do what you say? Let me repeat that: *All that Satan can do is what you say.* We have a tendency to be on the defensive where Satan is concerned, but in reality, we are on the offensive. After we become new creatures in Christ Jesus, *Satan has no authority over us except what we give him with the words of our mouths.* With your words, you either resist or comply with Satan's demands. With your words, you either resist or comply with God's Word. You are in command. The decision is yours. Nobody makes it for you. Satan is an outlaw. He has to steal man's authority in order to operate.

When you begin applying your faith for something, Satan goes to work in order to convince you to stop the force of faith that says, "I can have what I say according to Mark 11:23. I believe that I have received it." He has to stop your faith action, or what you have prayed will come to pass. Somehow he has to convince you that what you have believed is not coming to pass. *He deceives you in order to make you think you did not receive.*

Satan applies the necessary pressure within his limit. Most of the time, it doesn't take much pressure. A believer who is weak in God's Word will quickly say at the first symptom, "I guess I didn't get my healing. I still hurt." One believer may stand fast for a few days, while another will hold out for a few weeks, but it is the same costly mistake whether you have been believing for five days or five years. When you "throw in the towel" in the arena of faith, you become faithless to God's Word. You have just accepted your defeat.

"If we are faithless [do not believe and are untrue to Him], He remains true (faithful to His Word and His righteous character), for He cannot deny Himself" (2 Timothy 2:13, AMPC).

Why does it take a long time to have one prayer answered while the next prayer gets quick results? The most prevalent reason is the lack of knowledge of God's Word. The more revelation knowledge you have, the more accurate you are in believing God. When you are not acting in faith, the big WHY will slow you down and cause you to begin to operate in the natural.

When you begin to "wonder," look out! Unbelief is at your door. *I wonder why it is taking so long? I wonder why God hasn't done something by now? I wonder where I missed it?*

I learned from Norvel Hayes that wondering is a wavering. I had never really identified it before I heard him teach. *Wondering is wavering.* Think about that until you will never forget it, and you can avoid the "wonder trap." *Wondering is wavering.* According to James 1:6, we are to ask in faith, *nothing wavering.* When you waver, Satan can push you around. The next verse says that if you waver, don't even think you will receive anything of the Lord (James 1:6-7). *You can waver or you can receive. You cannot waver and receive at the same time.*

Let's be accurate about what we are saying. We are tempted to waver not when our prayer is answered, but when we are unable to see the result with our eyes and hear it with our ears and feel it with our body. *You believed that you received your answer when you prayed.* Your prayer was answered the moment you released your faith. The force of faith went to work to bring about the desire of your heart and mouth. That force of faith will continue to work until you can see the result in the physical or until you stop faith from operating with the words of your mouth. Your prayer is immediately taken care of in the world of the spirit. You have the answer if you do not become double-minded and waver. The world you can see, hear and touch will conform to the world of the spirit. Your prayer is answered when you pray, but you must exert the force of patience concerning your request until it is manifested—clearly visible to the eye or obvious to the understanding; appearing to the senses.

The moment you pray in faith, the angels go to work in the unseen realm of the spirit to bring your prayer to pass.

Let's look into this unseen world and see our angels at work!

OUR ANGELS AT WORK!

A re they not all ministering spirits, sent forth to minister for them who shall be heirs of salvation?" (Hebrews 1:14). The angels of God have been sent to minister for the heirs. "Christ hath redeemed us from the curse of the law, being made a curse for us...that the blessing of Abraham might come on the Gentiles through Jesus Christ; that we might receive the promise of the Spirit through faith.... And if ye be Christ's, then are ye Abraham's seed, and heirs according to the promise" (Galatians 3:13-14, 29).

The angels have been sent to minister for the heirs of the promise of Abraham (Genesis 17). The angels of God have been sent to perform whatever is necessary to establish God's promise on the earth. *The angels are assigned to administer (enforce) the blessing of Abraham to his seed in the current generation.* Just as surely as God established His covenant with Isaac, He is obligated by His own Word to establish His covenant with you. "If ye be Christ's, then are ye Abraham's seed"! Glory to God! If you have made Jesus the Lord of your life, then you are the seed of

> "PUT ON GOD'S WHOLE ARMOR [THE ARMOR OF A HEAVY-ARMED SOLDIER WHICH GOD SUPPLIES], THAT YOU MAY BE ABLE SUCCESSFULLY TO STAND UP AGAINST [ALL] THE STRATEGIES AND THE DECEITS OF THE DEVIL."
>
> Ephesians 6:11, AMPC

Abraham and heir to his blessing.

The angels are to administer the New Covenant (which is the fulfillment of the Old Covenant) to the heirs of promise. In scripture from Genesis to Revelation, you see the angels administering God's covenant to Abraham and his seed. Galatians 3:19 says that the law was *ordained by angels*. W. E. Vine states that this word is used in the sense of *administered*. The dictionary defines *administer* as to "have charge of as chief agent in managing." It gives these synonyms of *administer*: "manage, conduct, minister, furnish, supply, dispense, distribute, direct, control, execute, superintend." Through the Old and New Covenants, you can see the angels at work doing these very things.

Young's Analytical Concordance shows the word *angel* to be "messenger or agent." Angels are CIA—Covenant Inforcing Agents. (The spelling is not too good, but the message is great!) The angels are God's agents to see that His Word, His Covenant, is fulfilled in the earth. "Bless (affectionately, gratefully praise) the Lord, you His angels, you mighty ones who do His commandments, hearkening to the voice of His word. Bless (affectionately, gratefully praise) the Lord, all you His hosts, you His ministers who do His pleasure" (Psalm 103:20-21, AMPC).

The angels are God's ministers to do His pleasure. Psalm 35:27, AMPC, says, "Let the Lord be magnified, Who takes pleasure in the prosperity of His servant." Glory to God. The angels do God's pleasure and His pleasure is the prosperity of His covenant men! The angels are in the earth to prosper you.

Hebrews 1:14 tells us that these angels have been sent; they are here. Hebrews 12:22 tells us that their number is innumerable. *The Amplified Bible, Classic Edition*, says countless multitudes of angels. Revelation 5:11, speaking of angels, says, "And they numbered ten thousand times ten thousand and thousands of thousands."

Hilton Sutton shared with us recently that as nearly as he can figure that would be one hundred trillion angels! A trillion is a million million millions. One hundred trillion (in numbers) is 100,000,000,000,000. Wow! I believe that is enough to establish God's covenant in the earth. There is no shortage of angel power. Brother Sutton said, "If there were five billion people on earth and they all got saved, we would still have 20,000 angels to minister to each of us. If half of the population of five billion were born again and the angels were distributed evenly, there would be 40,000 angels assigned to each heir." Brother Sutton's arithmetic helped me to realize just how many angels there are. To me, that is exciting!

The king of Syria sent horses, chariots, and a great army to seize the prophet Elisha. (One prophet was a threat to a nation!) "When the servant of the man of God rose early and went out, behold, an army with horses and chariots was around the city. Elisha's servant said to him, Alas, my master! What shall we do? [Elisha] answered, Fear not; for those with us are more than those with them.

Then Elisha prayed, Lord, I pray You, open his eyes that he may see. And the Lord opened the young man's eyes, and he saw, and behold, the mountain was full of horses and chariots of fire round about Elisha" (2 Kings 6:15-17, AMPC). The mountain was full of angels! Elisha's angels were ready to enforce the covenant of God. He had enough angels to take care of a "great army." There is no shortage of angels.

For the most part, the heirs of the promise have not been using the angel power available to them. There are so many angels that you are certain to have more than enough to get the job done, no matter what you exercise faith for in the Word of God. God is able and mighty to perform the Word! You do the believing, God will do the performing. You believe—God will establish!

The angels of God have been assigned to you as an heir of the promise. Their assignment is to establish God's promise to Abraham in your circumstances and life. In short, they are to prosper you as they prospered Abraham.

See yourself in this situation. You have 20,000 to 100,000 men (just natural men) working to prosper you. If these men work only eight hours a day at no charge to you, how long do you think it would take them to make you wealthy? Of course, you would have to be willing to let them work and not hinder them from fulfilling their assignments. Well, if a multitude of men operating in the natural could make you prosperous, what can the angels of God do who operate in the supernatural wisdom of God? God has made provision for us that is beyond our comprehension. Ephesians 3:20 speaks of our God as "him that is able to do *exceeding* abundantly above all that we ask or think, according to the power that worketh in us." God has promised to multiply Abraham's seed *exceedingly* and to be a God to them. We have been delighted just to receive what we have asked for, but according to this, God has covenanted and is able to do much, much more than we can ask or think!

I believe in these last days that we are going to rely on our inheritance of Abraham's blessing and exceed our natural thinking. (*Exceed*: "to be able to go beyond the given or supposed limit, measure or quantity.") In the past we have limited God's ability and willingness to bless us by setting a "supposed limit." "Oh, that would be too much to receive." One believer's "supposed limit" may be considerably greater than another's, but what I am sharing with you from the Word of God is that THERE IS NO LIMIT! God's promise to Abraham has no limit. It is as limitless as God Himself. The Bible says that Abraham was *extremely* rich and that the Lord had blessed him in *all* things. That is just all the words we have to describe his condition of blessing. (*Extreme*: "going to great lengths; very great or greatest; utmost in degree; of the best that can exist in reality or in imagination; excessive; immoderate.")

If you are the seed of Abraham, all that is required of you to enjoy the covenant provisions is obedience to God's Word. These provisions became yours through faith in Jesus Christ (Galatians 3:22). "Know therefore that the Lord thy God, he is God, the faithful God, which keepeth covenant and mercy with them that love him and keep his commandments to a thousand generations" (Deuteronomy 7:9).

Years ago we made the decision to be obedient to God's Word, and we have prospered; but today, I have decided to "go beyond any supposed limit" and allow God to multiply me *exceedingly*. I am an heir to His promise! You can continue to limit God if you want to, but I am willing to be blessed exceedingly beyond what I can ask or think (and I am very good at asking and thinking!).

I am believing God to establish His covenant with me in my generation. I have become *willing* to receive the blessing of Abraham in my time. I will not limit God to what I can ask or think. I release my faith to walk in the exceeding portion of the promise. I stagger not at the promise of God through unbelief. I am fully persuaded that what He has promised, He is also able to perform (Romans 4:20-21). This establishes my part of receiving.

Allow Your Angels to Work

"Are they not all ministering spirits, sent forth to minister for them who shall be heirs of salvation?" (Hebrews 1:14). The word *salvation* denotes "deliverance, preservation and soundness." Your words put the angels to work on your behalf to bring to pass whatever you say. The angels have been sent to establish God's covenant in your life. When you confess the Word of God over a situation, you put your angels to work. Yes, you have angels assigned to you. The words of your mouth bind them or loose them to work for you. If you speak faith words enforced by God's Word, your angels are free to bring about what you want to come to pass. "Bless (affectionately, gratefully praise) the Lord, you His angels, you mighty ones who do His commandments, hearkening to the voice of His word" (Psalm 103:20, AMPC). When you keep God's Word in your mouth, you keep your angels working to bring to pass whatever you say.

The angels are waiting on your words. The angels cannot work against our words. They will not work without words. Even in the Old Covenant, the angel told Daniel, "thy words were heard, and *I am come for thy words*" (Daniel 10:12). Daniel's words put the angel to work for him. Of course, our angels are freer to work now than in Daniel's day because Jesus defeated Satan. Satan does not have the authority he had before Jesus stripped him of all his power and authority. The angels have already been sent. They have been sent to minister for those who are heirs. They are here NOW! "And if ye be Christ's, then are ye Abraham's seed, and heirs according to the promise" (Galatians 3:29).

The words of your mouth bind Satan or loose him. The words of your mouth bind the angels or loose them. Your words control your destiny. Your life right now is the product of your words.

Remember, the key to receiving the desires of your heart is to make the words of your mouth agree with what you want. Do not speak words that are contrary to your will.

Charles Capps says, "God's Word is His will to man. Man's words should be his will toward God. The angels know this, so they listen to your words, then they move busily about to cause it to come to pass or allow it to come to pass. The Spirit of God spoke to me and said, 'If you speak sickness, disease, calamity, and bad things, the angels will surely not bring it to pass, nor cause it to come to pass. They will bow their heads, back off, and fold their hands, for you have bound them by the words of your mouth, and they cannot work for you. They will allow all the bad and evil to come to pass that you speak because your words are their warrant, and when you speak against their work, they cannot perform it.'" (The angels of God will never work to bring to pass words that support Satan's work.)

The moment you exercise faith in your covenant, the angels go to work to minister the result of your faith to you. The Bible says that they excel in strength. They are capable beings. They are spiritual beings. You cannot see them work. You cannot tell how much they have accomplished on your behalf, but you can believe God's Word and know that they are doing their job. Their job is to minister for you. They are not doing anything else. The angels work 24 hours a day. If you will speak God's Word and speak only the words you want to come to pass, the angels will work for you constantly.

There may be no evidence in the natural world that you are one step closer to receiving your answer one minute before it is manifested. Look at what took place with Kenneth and me when we released our faith for a home. There was no evidence that *anything* happened for years. The money was not in the bank. From looking at the bank account, it looked as though it might be the millennium before we moved in. We knew better than to look at the bank account. We knew to look to God's Word and not to circumstances. The thing I could not see was that when we released our faith, a woman started building our home, one that just fit our needs. All the time I could see no evidence that our house was being built. We continued to stand in faith without wavering, and we lived in that home for many years. The point is that the angels were working from the moment we began to exercise faith by speaking with our mouths. They hearkened to the voice of God's Word on our lips.

Remember that you can only see the result of your faith after it is completed.

Your last words are the controlling factor. If you speak of things that are not as though they were for five years, two months, and three days, but on the fourth day of the fifth year in the second month, you allow your words to speak contrary to what you desire to come to pass, the last words you speak become the law in force and begin to create the situation. You have wavered. "But let him ask in faith, nothing wavering. For he that wavereth is like a wave of the sea driven with the wind and tossed. For let not that man think that he shall receive any thing of the Lord. A double minded man is unstable in all his ways" (James 1:6-8).

But I have good news! It works just as fast in your favor. You can change your words from negative to positive as quickly as you can from positive to negative. Immediately take authority over words that defeat your faith. If you have spoken those words of doubt and fear, you can quickly amend them. Render those words powerless to come to pass. Negate them in the Name of Jesus and reinstate what you want to come to pass. Your last words either put the angels to work or force them to step back, bow their heads, and fold their hands. Your angels are waiting for you to give them words to bring to pass. They have been sent forth to minister for you. Turn the angels loose to work in your behalf by continually speaking what you want to come to pass in your life. Your words put into motion your circumstances, the affairs of your life, the condition of your body, your acceptance or rejection by other people.

God's Word is His will. If your words are not your will, you will be disappointed in life because your words will come to pass.

Remember, the key to receiving the desires of your heart is to make the words of your mouth agree with what you want.

YES, YOU CAN STAND!

In conclusion, be strong in the Lord [be empowered through your union with Him]; draw your strength from Him [that strength which His boundless might provides]. Put on God's whole armor [the armor of a heavy-armed soldier which God supplies], that you may be able successfully to stand up against [all] the strategies and the deceits of the devil.... Therefore put on God's complete armor, that you may be able to resist and stand your ground on the evil day [of danger], and, having done all [the crisis demands], to stand.... Stand therefore" (Epheisans 6:10-11, 13-14, AMPC).

And having done all to stand. STAND! We are admonished to put on God's whole armor. According to this scripture, with His armor we can successfully stand against all the strategies and deceits of Satan. We are told to put on God's armor so that we can resist and stand our ground when Satan comes to attack. "And having done all to stand. Stand therefore." Yes, you can do it. God's Word says that you can. You are strong in the Lord if you have God's Word in your heart. Lift up the shield of faith with which you can quench all the fiery darts of the wicked

> "THE BLESSING
> OF THE LORD,
> IT MAKETH RICH,
> AND HE ADDETH
> NO SORROW
> WITH IT."
>
> Proverbs 10:22

one (verse 16). This word from the Lord tells you that *you* can quench every fiery dart that Satan sends your way. *You!* God has given you His armor. Your Bible is God speaking to *you*. *Your shield of faith is the words of your mouth.* This shield of faith is able to stop every fiery dart, every attack from Satan.

How long do you stand? How long does this verse say to stand? Three days? Three months? Three years? Three decades? Three centuries? Praise God, it does not say how long. The Bible just says, "Having done *all* to stand. STAND THEREFORE."

Don't attempt to go after something in faith without first making a quality decision to be willing to keep faith applied until the result is completed. You cannot succeed by *trying* to receive by faith. Trying will not produce. Commit yourself and all that you are without reservation to the fact that God's Word is true. Make this declaration: "His Word does not fail. God's Word will come to pass in my life. I will not faint and lose courage. I will do all to stand, and therefore I will stand. I am like a tree planted by the water. I shall not be moved by circumstances, people or Satan. I stand on God's Word. I will succeed and not fail. I will win and not lose. I am far from the thought of oppression or destruction, for I shall not fear."

When you fight the good fight of faith, be determined to win.

The Power of Patience

After you have prayed the will of God, have said with your mouth what you desire, and have believed that you have received, be ready to exert the force of patience until your faith produces the answer in the seen world.

Patience undergirds faith and keeps faith applied until the result is manifested in the earth. When you learn to release the power of patience, you can receive anything from God that agrees with His Word. Frankly, this is where most people fail when attempting to walk by faith, but *it doesn't have to be so*. Patience is the difference between *trying* and *doing*. Some people *go fishing* and others *catch fish*. Some *attempt* to walk by faith, others *succeed*. *Patience makes the difference*.

Kenneth Copeland says, "The power of patience is a working force. When faith has a tendency to waver, it is patience that comes to faith's aid to make it stand. The power of patience is necessary to undergird faith. Faith and patience are frequently mentioned together in the Bible. Faith and patience are the power twins. Together, they will produce every time. Patience without faith has no substance. On the other hand, many times faith without patience, after a while, will fail to stand firm on the evidence of God's Word. Without the power of patience at work, we will allow sense knowledge—the things we see—to overwhelm our faith. We should base our faith on what the Word says rather than on what our natural eye can see. Patience undergirds faith and gives it endurance to persevere until the answer comes. Faith is a powerful force. It always works. It is not that our faith is weak and needs strength, but without the power of patience, we ourselves stop the force of faith with negative confession and action" (*The Force of Faith*).

Do not, therefore, fling away your fearless confidence, for it carries a great and glorious compensation of reward. For *you have need of steadfast patience and endurance,* so that you may perform and fully accomplish the will of God, and thus receive and carry away [and enjoy to the full] what is promised.... But the just shall live by faith [My righteous servant shall live by his conviction respecting man's relationship to God and divine things, and holy fervor born of faith and conjoined with it]; and if he draws back and shrinks in fear, My soul has no delight or pleasure in him. But our way is not that of those who draw back to eternal misery (perdition) and are utterly destroyed, but we are of those who believe [who cleave to and trust in and rely on God through Jesus Christ, the Messiah] and by faith preserve the soul. Now *faith is the assurance* (the confirmation, the title deed) of the things [we] hope for, being the proof of things [we] do not see and the conviction of their reality [faith perceiving as real fact what is not revealed to the senses] (Hebrews 10:35-11:1, AMPC).

"You have need of steadfast patience and endurance." W.E. Vine says "patience is the quality that does not surrender to circumstances or succumb under trial: it is the opposite of despondency and is associated with hope." The dictionary defines *despondency* as "to be cast down; to lose courage, confidence, or hope." Patience and despondency are opposite forces. Satan uses despondency against you to stop the power of patience as he uses fear to stop faith. Patience is a godly force that comes from your spirit; despondency is a satanic force that attacks your soul— your mind, will and emotions.

Patience encourages fearless confidence in God's Word despite contrary evidence in the seen world. Fearless confidence that God's Word never fails when relied on in faith will produce great and glorious results. When Satan brings a test or trial against you, do not fling away your confidence in God's Word. This refusal to cast away your confidence in God's Word is the power of patience at work.

"Blessed...is the man whom You discipline and instruct, O Lord, and teach out of Your law, that You may give him power to keep himself calm in the days of adversity, until the [inevitable] pit of corruption is dug for the wicked" (Psalm 94:12-13, AMPC). *Patience is the power to hold yourself calm.* According to this scripture, it is the result of being instructed by God's Word and being obedient to that Word—being a doer of the Word and not a hearer only (James 1:22).

The power of patience is released to work for you in the face of adversity when you act on what you know the Word of God says about your situation. You are saying, "Adversity, you don't count. God's Word says that you are defeated and under my feet. God's Word is true, regardless of what I see with my natural eye. God's Word has great and glorious reward. I am holding fast to that Word, and I will not fling it away."

In the face of adversity when it looks like doom is inevitable, Satan puts strong pressure on you to faint and give up. At that moment, you want to succumb to the pressure and let go of God's Word. Don't do it! YOU

CANNOT SUCCUMB TO SATAN'S PRESSURE
WITHOUT FLINGING AWAY YOUR CONFIDENCE
IN GOD'S WORD. To act on Satan's pressure, you have
to quit acting on God's Word that says you have received
the answer. There is no middle ground. When it comes to
standing on God's Word in faith, you are either on or off.

Patience has the courage to refuse what Satan, circumstances and people can prove true in the natural world.
Patience says, "Let God be true and every man a liar!
I will not succumb to pressure. I am moved by nothing
except the Word of God." When Satan's pressure says that
God's Word is not working, patience rejects it as a lie.
Patience has no fear. Patience knows that God's Word has
never failed in thousands of years. Patience knows that
when faith is exercised to receive God's Word, success is
inevitable. Patience knows that the pit of corruption is
already dug for the wicked. (Satan is trying to get you to
jump into the pit that has already been dug for him. The
answer to that is simple: *Don't do it!*)

James 1:4 gives an insight into the great and glorious
compensation of fearless confidence in God's Word and
His ability. "But let patience have her perfect work, that
ye may be perfect and entire, wanting nothing." Glory
to God! That is great compensation—perfect and entire,
wanting nothing. Kenneth and I can be witnesses to that.
God has blessed us with every earthly and heavenly blessing that we have desired and more besides. We know from
experience that fearless confidence in the Word of God
causes you to be "perfectly and fully developed...lacking in
nothing" (James 1:4, AMPC). Of course, the Word has only
begun to produce in our lives what is available to us. We

have just scratched the surface, but we intend to diligently *keep scratching*. We are dedicated to the Word of God.

Looking back at the condition we were in when we found out that the Word is true and can be depended on to meet our needs, it is apparent that we have come a long way. Yet, we are so aware that we have not even made a dent in the great things God has for those who love Him and honor His Word. We started out with nothing—thousands of dollars in debt, no steady income, past-due bills with threat of a lawsuit, an old worn-out Oldsmobile, a rented two-bedroom house on the Arkansas River furnished in "early Goodwill."

Someone said that you shouldn't jump out of the boat until you are ready to walk on the water. He was talking about using your faith where you are right now. When he said it, I thought, *That is good advice, but Kenneth and I were in the water, sinking fast, when we first heard the good news that God's Word would get us out.* The Word of God was our life preserver! We made the decision to do exactly what we saw in the Word of God. We made the decision to act on God's Word and started searching for some Word to act on. What a wonderful and blessed experience it has been!

Our life is no longer limited to what is common to man. We have learned to depend on the supernatural—our Father—instead of the beggarly elements of this world. The world's system is seriously deficient, but the heavenly system has the answer for every need. *The Bible secret to operating on the heavenly system is to fearlessly act on God's Word.* "Do not, therefore, fling away your fearless confidence, for it carries a great and glorious compensation of reward."

"But the just shall live by faith...and if he draws back and shrinks in fear, My soul has no delight or pleasure in him." To live by faith is to have your very existence dependent on faith. The living of your life is to be done by faith—every aspect of living dependent on faith in God's Word.

If you draw back from the Word of God and shrink in the fear that God's Word is not working in your life, God will still love you, but He will have no *pleasure* in you. "But without faith it is impossible to please him; for he that cometh to God must believe that he is, and that he is a rewarder of them that diligently seek him" (Hebrews 11:6). It is impossible to please God without faith. If you are going to please God, *you must operate in faith*. Faith not only believes that God exists but that God rewards those who diligently seek Him. Why can God take no pleasure in you if you draw back in fear? Because God takes pleasure in the prosperity of His people. "Fear not, little flock; for it is your Father's good pleasure to give you the kingdom" (Luke 12:32). *The instant you draw back in fear*, you quit operating in faith—you quit pleasing God, *you quit believing that God is the rewarder*. When you stopped the operation of faith, you quit believing that God is the rewarder. When you stopped the operation of faith, you shut the door to God's blessing. He takes pleasure in your prosperity, not your defeat. "Let them shout for joy, and be glad, that favour my righteous cause: yea, let them say continually, Let the Lord be magnified, which hath pleasure in the prosperity of his servant" (Psalm 35:27). These witnesses from the Word should establish in your thinking that God gets pleasure from prospering covenant men.

We are believers, not doubters. We are not of those who draw back and are destroyed; we are believers and by faith preserve the soul. *By faith preserve the soul* is not speaking of preserving the heart of man (the spirit), but of preserving the soul of man—his mind, will and emotions. Faith, undergirded by the power of patience, defends and protects the soul from Satan's attack and his pressure to draw back in fear. Faith is the assurance of the things that we believe we have received. *Faith in God's Word is our proof that we have received, even though we cannot yet see it with our natural eye.* Your soul is where Satan rages against you with doubt, defeat and discouragement. Faith with patience will preserve that stronghold and give Satan no place in your life. *You have the power to hold yourself calm.*

Satan attacks every believer who attempts to walk by faith. He uses the same tactics on all of us. He has no more right of authority over one than another. He has nothing more to use against you than he has to use against me. "There hath no temptation taken you but such as is common to man: but God is faithful, who will not suffer you to be tempted above that ye are able; but will with the temptation also *make a way to escape*, that ye may be able to bear it" (1 Corinthians 10:13). Tradition reads this verse as saying God will let you suffer (individually, in each trial) to your breaking point, and when He is sure that you can take no more, He will provide an answer that you can tolerate.

Jesus said that tradition makes the Word of no effect. We are not obligated to tradition. We are free to rightly divide the Word by the Spirit of God.

SATAN IS BOUND BY THE LAWS OF GOD. He can bring no trial to you that you cannot overcome with

God's Word. He has no weapon that is not subject to the Word of God. God has given Satan an ultimatum where tempting you is concerned. Satan is already bound by the laws of God. God will not allow (suffer) Satan to go beyond the limit he has in the earth to try your faith. Satan would not dare go beyond what God has decreed, nor does he have the power within his reach to do so. You are able to overcome and be victorious over every temptation and trial. In God's Word, you have already been given the authority to overcome every temptation and trial that Satan can bring against you (2 Peter 1:4). *God has already provided you that way of escape.*

"That ye may be able to bear it" means that, with the steadfast patience admonished in Hebrews 10:36, you can bear (endure) Satan's pressure to yield to circumstances without surrendering to that pressure—performing and fully accomplishing the will of God, and thus receive and carry away what is promised. "Blessed is the man that endureth temptation...he shall receive..." (James 1:12).

Our Weapons Are Not Carnal

"For though we walk in the flesh, we do not war after the flesh: (For the weapons of our warfare are not carnal, but mighty through God to the pulling down of strong holds;) casting down imaginations, and every high thing that exalteth itself against the knowledge of God, and bringing into captivity every thought to the obedience of Christ" (2 Corinthians 10:3-5).

Our weapons are not carnal! Our weapons are not limited to what is common to man. Satan is limited and can bring no temptation or trial against you that is not common to man. The weapons of Satan's arsenal are limited, but *we* are not limited to what is common to man. The weapons of our warfare are mighty through God to the pulling down of strongholds. We have God's power behind us. Whose strongholds are these that our weapons are so powerful in pulling down? Satan's! While Satan is limited in his attack against you, you are backed by the power of God; and all that Satan can do does not begin to tax God's ability and power.

The same Greek word *peirasmos* is translated "temptations, tests, and trials." When Satan tempts (pressures) you to back off God's Word, he is trying your faith (James 1:3). Because of Satan, you have the opportunity to *prove* (also the same Greek word) that you believe God's Word is true. Satan can challenge God's Word, but God's Word can pass the test!

James 1:14 says that "every man is tempted, when he is drawn away of his own lust, and enticed." When James said *every* man, he did not leave you out. You are tempted when you are drawn away from God's Word. *Lust is desire inconsistent with the will of God, which is the Word of God; lust is of the mind* (W. E. Vine). Satan attempts to lure (entice) you away from what God's Word says. For Satan to get anywhere with you in temptation, he has to first draw you away from God's Word. "Let him ask in faith, nothing wavering" (James 1:6).

If you refuse to give place in your mind and in your words to that which is contrary to God's Word, Satan's temptations, tests and trials cannot influence your affairs. Satan cannot work in your life apart from fear any more than God can work without faith. If you refuse to fear that God's Word will not work, you give Satan nothing to work with. He has to have your cooperation, your consent.

If you are faithful and steadfast in God's Word, you can count it all joy when you fall into different temptations (James 1:2). They will not affect you.

"We do not war after flesh." If the war is not in the flesh, then where is it? Where are the imaginations? Where are the thoughts? IN THE MIND. The mind is scripturally called "the soul." The soul of man is his mind, his will, and his emotions. Satan's warfare against us is in this soulish realm. Through the mind, the will, and the emotions, Satan attacks the other areas of life. The mind is where the door to Satan is opened or shut. It is like the entry hall of a house where admission to the rest of the house is granted or refused.

Man is a spirit. He has a soul. He lives in a body (1 Thessalonians 5:23). When you made Jesus the Lord of your life, you—the spirit—were re-created and made a new creature (2 Corinthians 5:17). Your soul and body remained the same. The spirit of man is made to have dominion over the mind and body. The Bible tells us that the mind is to be renewed by the Word of God and the body is to be brought under subjection to God's Word. "I beseech you therefore, brethren, by the mercies of God, that ye present your bodies a living sacrifice, holy, acceptable unto God, which is your reasonable service. And be not conformed to this world: but be ye transformed by the renewing of your mind, that ye may prove what is that good, and acceptable, and perfect, will of God" (Romans 12:1-2). This says *brethren*. It is written to believers. We are to present our bodies a living sacrifice. We are not to be conformed to this world, but we are to be transformed by the renewing of our minds.

Christians who do not know what God's Word says about them are unable to live and enjoy privileges that already belong to them. Their minds have never been renewed to walk in the spirit; therefore, they continue to walk after the dictates of their flesh, or body (Galatians 5:16-17). But when the mind is renewed to God's Word, the outer life is transformed.

Satan attacks in the soulish realm: The mind that has not been renewed to the Word of God does not know it has a choice but to receive what Satan is offering it. The unrenewed mind does not know that there is an alternative. A believer has at his disposal all of the spiritual weapons in heaven's arsenal, but if his mind has never been renewed, he does not know that there is an arsenal—much less how to use the weapons. He is at Satan's mercy, and Satan has no mercy. What a pitiful position for a believer who has already been given all authority and power! "Why did that happen to Sister Smith? She was such a sweet Christian." The answer to *Why?* is always *unbelief*. The Bible tells us *why* God's people are sick, broke, tormented by fear, oppressed, and *why* they die young. "My people are destroyed for lack of knowledge" (Hosea 4:6).

Satan works on you the same way he worked on Eve. He tries to discredit God's Word in your mind. He has no authority. First Peter 5:8 says that Satan goes around as a roaring lion, seeking whom he may devour. He talks big, but bluff is all he has going for him. Notice, it says he walks about *as a roaring lion*. It doesn't say he is one. Jesus is the Lion of the tribe of Judah! He is our Lord. Jesus called Satan a liar and said that there is no truth in him "....because there is no truth in him. When he speaketh a lie, he speaketh of his own: for he is a liar, and the father of it" (John 8:44). Satan conceived lies and he is a master at it. Deception is all he has to use against the Body of Christ.

This is one place where the old phrase, "Where there's smoke, there's fire," does not apply. Satan is ALL smoke. Today we use the phrase "blowing smoke." That's what Satan is doing! He is "blowing smoke" at you to make you believe that God's Word is not true. *He has to trick you into using your own authority against yourself.*

SATAN WANTS YOUR WORDS. In order to be successful, he has to deceive you into speaking words that will stop your faith. He works on your mind, your will, and your emotions to achieve his desired result. Once you realize how Satan has been defeating you, there is no reason to continue allowing him to use the same bag of tricks again and again. He only has one bag. He uses the same tactics over and over. You must use the weapons of your warfare as persistently as Satan uses his.

Jesus tells us that when the Word is sown, Satan comes immediately to take away the Word that was sown in the heart. Satan will try your faith when you make a stand on the Word. He comes to influence you to say what he wants to come to pass. This is contrary to what you believe that you have received. When Satan comes to steal the Word out of your heart, don't let him have it. Stand fast on the Word, and don't be moved by pressure to give in. Satan can *only* do what you say. *Satan is bound by the laws of God.* He is bound by the law of God that says *you* can have whatsoever you say.

"And having spoiled principalities and powers, he made a show of them openly, triumphing over them in it" (Colossians 2:15). Jesus stripped Satan of the authority and power Adam gave him. *The Amplified Bible, Classic Edition* says, "[God] disarmed the principalities and powers that were ranged against us." *Moffatt's Translation* speaks of the *dethroned powers* who rule this world (1 Corinthians 2:6). Satan is dethroned! *So how does he exercise control over men's lives?* Through ignorance. Most people don't know that Satan has been dethroned. Once you recognize that he is a defeated foe and that you have been given authority over him in the Name of Jesus, you realize that Satan can *only* do what you allow him to do. You have the power and authority to give him no place in your life.

Satan operates in the soulish realm. Your soul is composed of your mind, will, and emotions. When Satan brings pressure to bear on your mind, use the Name of Jesus to cast him out. Dethroned, he has to adhere to that Name spoken in faith from the lips of a believer (another law of God to which Satan is bound). If Satan is attacking your mind with doubt, fear or despondency, speak to it in the Name of Jesus and command its operation against you to cease. "Fear, in the Name of Jesus, I break your power to operate against me, and I command you to leave my presence."

In a typical attack from fear, Satan will pressure you to accept this: "You are not going to get your healing this time. You don't have a headache like you thought; you have a tumor of the brain. You are going to die. Your time has come. Panic! Get help! Call the doctor! Tell him you believe that you have a brain tumor."

Wow! Can you see how that rat works? God's Word says Jesus bore your sicknesses and carried your diseases and by His stripes you were healed. Satan has replaced God's Word with fear of sickness. If you fall for his tricks and say that you believe you have a brain tumor, you have allowed Satan to steal the Word of God from your heart.

You might think it would be obvious that Satan was only trying to deceive, but it is not nearly as obvious to a man unfamiliar with Satan's mode of operation—neither does he think as rationally when his head is splitting with pain. Satan may have been working on that person for nine months to receive a tumor of the brain.

Obviously, Satan will try to sell you something that he thinks you will buy. He knows you. He has worked on you for years. He knows your case history. Maybe you would buy a heart attack. "Hey, pal, that's not indigestion. You are getting ready to have a heart attack. Feel that pain in your arm? It's a symptom of heart failure. You are overweight. You have been under pressure. (He ought to know that is where the pressure came from.) You have been worrying about your finances day and night. It has just been too much for your heart. You know that it is appointed to every man a time to die. Get your affairs in order. You don't have long to live. You don't want to leave your wife in a mess."

Satan is a cruel, merciless being. He doesn't care if you are three years old or 63 or 93. His ambition is to kill, steal and destroy. He will do it if you let him. Satan will pressure you into acting on fear and then condemn you for it. He will push you into a corner until you act on his demands and then turn to rend you. He will bring you under condemnation and use it against you as long as you let him.

You need to realize that one thing leads to another when you cooperate with Satan. He will try to get you in deeper and deeper. He doesn't play fair. He doesn't know "fair." Satan is an utterly corrupt, wicked and sadistic being. There are no human words that can adequately describe him. Don't allow yourself to serve him. Refuse to act on fear. Don't cooperate with doubt. Don't cooperate with despondency. Refuse to act on Satan's demands.

SATAN IS AFTER YOUR WORDS. SATAN IS AFTER YOUR WORDS. SATAN IS AFTER YOUR WORDS. SATAN IS AFTER YOUR WORDS. SATAN IS AFTER YOUR WORDS. Did you get that? SATAN IS AFTER YOUR WORDS. He has to have them in order to operate against you.

DEFEAT
SATAN'S
ATTACKS

The first step in defeating Satan's attack against you is *make the decision that you are not going to allow him to change your confession of faith that you believe you received when you prayed.* DECISION! Decision is the exercise of your will. The dictionary defines *will* as "strong purpose, intention, or determination." Isaiah said that if you are *willing* and obedient, you shall eat the fat of the land. Make an irrevocable decision of these things: *God's Word is true. I will act only in faith. I will speak only in faith. I have believed I receive.*

A fearless confession comes from a Word-ruled mind. Make the decision to cast down imaginations and every high thing that exalts itself against the Word of God. Make the decision to bring into captivity every thought to the obedience of

> "SO BE SUBJECT TO GOD. RESIST THE DEVIL [STAND FIRM AGAINST HIM], AND HE WILL FLEE FROM YOU."
>
> James 4:7,
> AMPC

Christ. "Neither give place to the devil" (Epheisans 4:27). Your mind is where you first have the choice of giving place to Satan or resisting him according to James 4:7, *The Amplified Bible, Classic Edition*, "So be subject to God. Resist the devil [stand firm against him], and he will flee from you."

We are to be subject to God and His Word. You cannot be subject to God and at the same time obey Satan's dictates. You are going to obey one or the other. You are going to act on God's Word and believe you have received, or you are going to act on the fear and doubt that Satan is pressuring you to receive in your mind.

The decision of your will—to stand and continue to stand, regardless of Satan's tactics and pressure—will enable you to accomplish the will of God and receive and carry away what is promised. Your decision will cause the power of patience to undergird your faith. Patience is the quality that does not surrender to circumstances. Patience operates at YOUR will. It does not operate for you at anyone else's will, not even God's. *You* determine your will in a situation.

Do not be willing to receive any imagination or high thing that Satan exalts against the knowledge of God's Word. If God's Word says you have the answer, don't let Satan take it from you. *Will* and *desire* differ at this point: To desire is to want something; to will is to determine to receive something.

Jerry Savelle calls this decision of your will "a right mental attitude." He says that a right mental attitude is vital when Satan is trying your faith. He gives Shadrach, Meshach and Abednego as an example. Now those three men knew they had a covenant. They said, "King, our God whom we serve is able to deliver us from the burning fiery furnace, and He will deliver us out of thine hand. But we will not serve your gods nor worship the golden image." They believed that God was able to deliver them, and they refused to compromise their covenant with God by bowing their knee to another god. *They would not bow and they did not burn.* There was no compromise in them. They went into the fire fully intending to come out.

Oh, the fire was hot—so hot that the men who put them into the furnace were killed by the heat. But Shadrach, Meshach and Abednego were covenant men! "And the princes, governors, and captains, and the king's counsellors, being gathered together, saw these men, upon whose bodies the fire had no power, nor was an hair of their head singed, neither were their coats changed, nor the smell of fire had passed on them" (Daniel 3:27). (Verse 28 is an example of angels enforcing the covenant.) Isn't that thrilling?

When you encounter temptations, tests and trials, *be determined* to come out without even the smell of defeat! This is a right mental attitude.

The second step in stopping Satan's attack to defeat your faith is RESIST THE DEVIL. *You resist him with the words of your mouth—the same way you submit to him.* "Submit yourselves therefore to God. Resist the devil, and he will flee from you" (James 4:7). You have submitted yourself to the obedience of God's Word; therefore, refuse to receive or give thought to anything that exalts itself against God's Word that says you have the petition you desired of Him.

Do what my daughter did to me when she was about three years old. I said, "Kellie, pick up your toys." She answered, as she walked away, "That's not my thought."

That's the way you have to do Satan. If it's doubt, defeat or discouragement, tell him: "THAT'S NOT MY THOUGHT!"

Give unbelief no place in your will, mind or emotions. Thoughts that rob you are thoughts of doubt, defeat, discouragement, lack, sickness and fear. These are always from Satan. Refuse to entertain thoughts that attack your faith in God's Word. Jesus said, "In my name shall they cast out devils" (Mark 16:17). Philippians 2:9-11 says, "Wherefore God also hath highly exalted him, and given him a name which is above every name: That at the name of Jesus every knee should bow, of things in heaven, and things in earth, and things under the earth; and that every tongue should confess that Jesus Christ is Lord, to the glory of God the Father." *Satan's knee must bow at the Name of Jesus spoken in faith by a believer.* The Name of Jesus is a powerful weapon in heaven's arsenal—it paralyzes Satan.

Speak aloud and say whatever is necessary to stop Satan's mental attack. "Satan, in the Name of Jesus, I resist you and I command you to stop your maneuvers against me and the Word of God. I will no longer tolerate doubt and unbelief. I bind you from operating against my mind. I will not receive anything contrary to the Word of God. Flee from my presence. I cast you out in the Name of Jesus."

Or say this: "Pain, in Jesus' Name, I command you to get out of my body. I will not allow anything in my mind or body that is contrary to God's Word. I resist sickness in the Name of Jesus."

Say, "Lack, I speak to you in Jesus' Name. I command you to get out of my life. I break your power over my affairs and forbid you to operate against me. Jesus came that I might have life and have it more abundantly. I am willing and obedient; so according to God's Word, I eat the fat of the land. I am *not* willing to live in lack. I am willing to live in abundance. I am an heir to the promise of Abraham. I am exceedingly blessed financially."

Whatever it takes to make you free, speak it out in the Name of Jesus and command it to come to pass. Speak the result that you desire. SATAN CAN ONLY DO WHAT YOU SAY. If you say, "FLEE!" he goes. If you agree with him against the Word of God, he stays.

Don't give your thought life to Satan's temptation. Don't dwell on his threats, just rebuke them. *Worry* is meditating on the words of the devil. Don't tolerate that. Meditate on God's Word. Resist the devil and resist him quickly. Don't allow him to hang around, pressuring your mind. At the first symptom of unbelief, command Satan to flee. At the first symptom of sickness, act on God's Word and resist sickness in Jesus' Name. At the first symptom of lack, command it to go. Do not procrastinate in spiritual things. Act immediately at the first sign of temptation. NEITHER GIVE PLACE TO THE DEVIL.

The third step in defeating Satan's attack is GIVE YOUR ATTENTION TO GOD'S WORD. According to Proverbs 4:20-23, "My son, attend to my words; incline thine ear unto my sayings. Let them not depart from thine eyes; keep them in the midst of thine heart. For they are life unto those that find them, and health to all their flesh. Keep thy heart with all diligence; for out of it are the issues of life." The more attention you give God's Word, the easier the other steps will be in resisting Satan's attacks.

Give your attention to the Word of God. Make your ears listen to God's Word. Keep God's Word in front of your eyes and in the midst of your heart. Satan tries to divert your attention from the Word to circumstances. God's Word says that abundance belongs to you. Satan says, "It does not. Look and see." When you are believing by faith, your circumstances usually are in agreement with Satan—and so are your friends. Satan wants your attention placed on things that are in agreement with him. Remember, patience is the quality that does not surrender to circumstances. The way you keep from being moved by what you see and by the negative circumstances surrounding you in the fight of faith is to continually give your attention to the Word of God.

Satan constantly sends you messages that say, "You do not have the answer, and you are not going to get the answer." He may use someone to call you on the phone, knock on you door, write you a letter, say it over TV, or he may just speak doubt to your mind. He is continually peddling doubt, defeat and unbelief. He is desperate. He has to make a sale or his commission is "0." HE WANTS YOUR ATTENTION OFF GOD'S WORD. If he can maneuver your attention from the Word, next you will begin to speak the words that will stop your faith. On the other hand, if you keep your attention on God's Word, he cannot find a foothold. You refuse to be drawn away from God's Word (James 1:14). You give Satan no place. You are continually meditating on what the Word says and are looking at it with your eyes and listening to it with your ears. He sends you "doubt bait" and you just say, "No, I resist that. It is contrary to the Word of God."

How does Satan sell his bad news to you?

Through your senses—what you can see, hear and feel. Proverbs tells you to keep your ear listening to the Word and to keep your eye looking at the Word. Oh, that makes you tough for Satan to handle!

Refuse to be moved by what you see—
be moved only by what God's Word says.

Refuse to be moved by what you hear—
be moved only by what God's Word says.

Refuse to be moved by circumstances—
be moved only by what God's Word says.

Refuse to be moved by what you feel—
be moved only by what God's Word says.

Let Satan's witnesses of defeat, doubt and failure bounce off of you like a rubber ball on the sidewalk. Don't even give them your attention. Just keep your eye centered on the Word.

"For which cause we faint not.... While we look not at the things which are seen, but at the things which are not seen: for the things which are seen are temporal; but the things which are not seen are eternal" (2 Corinthians 4:16, 18). You will not faint if you look in the right place. This scripture says to look not at things you can see with those two things on each side of your nose and between your ears.

We are admonished to look at things which are not seen. *How can you look at things which are not seen?* Through the eye of your spirit—the eye of faith (Epheisans 1:18). The eye of faith looks into the spirit world instead of the natural world. The eye of faith sees only

121

the covenant. The Word of God is evidence to the eye of faith whereas the circumstances are evidence to the natural eye. The eye of faith sees that the angels are working and that Satan is bound. The eye of faith sees what God sees according to His Word.

Learning to govern your affairs according to the eye of faith will cause you to prosper in all that you do. That is what God was teaching Joshua. "This book of the law shall not depart out of thy mouth; but thou shalt meditate therein day and night, that thou mayest observe to do according to all that is written therein: for then thou shalt make thy way prosperous, and then thou shalt have good success" (Joshua 1:8). *You* make your way prosperous. The words of your own mouth *make* your way prosperous.

Learn to look through that third eye—the eye of faith!

You can come to a place where you almost automatically *depend* on the eye of faith rather than what you see with your natural eye. It will become second nature to trust the eye of faith *more* than *your* natural eye. This is scriptural too. "But solid food is for full-grown men, for those whose senses and mental faculties are trained by practice to discriminate and distinguish between what is morally good and noble and what is evil and contrary either to divine or human law" (Hebrews 5:14, AMPC).

Yes, your senses can be trained on the Word of God. They are trained by practice—the practice of continually demanding them to act on God's Word. At first, your natural eyes will argue and say, *It isn't so! It isn't so! Look. Look. It isn't so.* But after a while, they will readjust and keep quiet, as much as to say, *I don't see it, but by experience I know it must be so if the Word says so.*

As my son John said after church one night when he was just a little boy, "Thank goodness, Daddy, we've got three eyes. I'm so glad we've got three eyes." He had just heard about the eye of faith—the eye that only looks at what God's Word says!

You can reach the place where you *never waver.*

YOU ARE KEEPING THAT WORD IN THE CENTER OF YOUR HEART. It is alive and working. The fruit of the Spirit is continually emanating from your spirit—love, joy, peace, patience, faith, goodness, kindness... How can Satan find any place in that? These forces come forth from the human spirit. Proverbs 4:23 says that we are to keep our heart with all diligence, for out of it are the issues (forces) of life. Be diligent about keeping your heart full of the Word of God.

When you are in a good meeting for three or four days hearing the Word taught daily, you can almost *feel* your spirit issuing those forces! You are so strong spiritually and the Word of God is working in you to such a degree that *you do not even consider being defeated.* Your heart is full of the Word of God. The reason you are so strong is that for several days you have been giving your attention day and night to God's Word. Your spirit is rising up within you, bringing forth whatever you need.

"Guard above all things, guard your inner self, for so you live and prosper; bar out all talk of evil, and banish wayward words" (Proverbs 4:23-24, *Moffatt*). Keeping your heart will get your body healed, make you prosper, cause you to walk in wisdom, and cause you to walk in faith.

Study the Word for yourself. Use tapes, meetings, newsletters, books, whatever, to feed your spirit with

God's Word. *Be diligent about keeping your heart full of God's Word.* It is difficult for Satan to even get your attention when you are full of the Word of God. You don't have time to pay attention to his bad news because you are thinking about God's Word. You can't think about two things at once!

The fourth step in overcoming Satan's temptation to receive the defeat of your faith is REFUSE TO SPEAK WORDS CONTRARY TO WHAT YOU BELIEVE YOU HAVE RECEIVED.

Continually speak the Word of God into the face of adversity. Satan is after your words so that he can use them against you. Refuse to let him influence your words. Speak words of faith. Speak the end result. Speak words of success. Speak words of abundance. Speak words of healing. You will have what you say. *Make your words agree with what you desire to come to pass.*

Satan's strongest weapon against faith is fear. Let's take the wraps off fear and see what there is to be afraid of. The dictionary defines *fear* as "that which is caused by intimidation of adversaries." *Intimidate* means "to force or deter with threats of violence."

How does Satan use fear? He comes to challenge what you have believed in God's Word. *He pressures you with threats to make you afraid to rely on God's Word.*

To intimidate is to make timid or to cow. He bombards your mind with unbelief until you begin to think, *What is going to happen to me if God's Word does not work?* He endeavors to make the fear of consequences of failure so great and heavy on your mind that you will cow down to him and no longer have the will to stand in determined faith.

Learn to answer every doubt immediately with the
Word of God. Learn to answer every fear with the Word
of God. The Word will cause fear to fall at your feet.
Learn to do combat with the Sword of the Spirit (Epheisans 6:17). The Sword of the Spirit is not carnal, but
mighty through God to the pulling down of strongholds.
Just be like Jesus when He was being tempted and say, "It is
written." Jesus was establishing His covenant as the seed of
Abraham. Satan has no defense for the Word of God.

All Satan can do is try to convince you that the Word
of God will not work for you. Refuse to act on fear. Fear
is Satan's weapon. Don't cooperate with Satan. "For God
hath not given us the spirit of fear; but of power, and of
love, and of a sound mind" (2 Timothy 1:7).

Refuse to allow Satan to intimidate you with threats.
He can *only* do what you say. He has no authority over
you unless you give it to him. As long as you give him no
place, he cannot carry out the first threat. It is when you
become timid and fearful with the words of your mouth
that Satan gains the upper hand. Do not allow fear to
make you compromise. What you compromise to keep,
you will lose. If you do not compromise the Word of God,
Satan is powerless to cause you harm. *If you won't bow,
you can't burn!* Satan can no more hurt you apart from
fear than God can bless you apart from faith. Satan is
bound by your covenant with God when you trust that
covenant to produce in your life. "The Lord is on my side;
I will not fear" (Psalm 118:6).

Turn fear out with the Word of God. "There is no
fear in love; but perfect love casteth out fear: because fear
hath torment. He that feareth is not made perfect in love"

(1 John 4:18). "And what this love consists in is this: that we live and walk in accordance with and guided by His commandments (His orders, ordinances, precepts, teaching). This is the commandment, as you have heard from the beginning, that you continue to walk in love [guided by it and following it]" (2 John 6, AMPC). Perfect love casts out fear. Satan cannot move perfect love with the fear of failure: *What is going to happen to me if God's Word doesn't work?* Love is acting on God's Word. "And this is love, that we walk after his commandments" (2 John 6). Love has already made the decision to be obedient to the Father regardless of the circumstances. Love says, "I will not rebel against the Word of my Father." Love knows that God's Word will bring success, never failure.

Love has no fear. Love keeps the covenant. Love has no reason to fear because love knows that God *will* establish His covenant with the heirs of promise who believe. Love knows the covenant-keeping God does not fail. There is no fear in love because there is no fear in faith. "Fear not, Abram, I am your Shield, your abundant compensation, and your reward shall be exceedingly great" (Genesis 15:1, AMPC).

If you allow fear to operate against you, you can expect despondency to come next. *Despondency* means "the loss of courage, confidence or hope." It is the opposite of patience. Oh, just give Satan an inch and he will take a mile. Invite him to dinner and he will bring his pajamas! Unless you plan to live a defeated life and be subject to Satan instead of God, you are going to have to resist Satan somewhere along the way. The sooner you resist temptation, the easier it will be. The longer you wait to exercise your authority, the more deeply Satan will become entrenched in your affairs. *Entertain fear and Satan will bless you with despondency.* Despondency moves in to convince you that there is no way out—a hopeless case. *You might as well just give in. Don't even try to resist. God's Word will not work.* Despondency says, "Why? Why did this happen to me? I have served God. I...I...I...."

The BIG I opens the door to self-pity. Self-pity says, "You have been so mistreated. Your loved ones don't care about you." If you believe that, then self-pity will say, "God doesn't care about you either. If He did, He wouldn't let you get in this shape." *He wouldn't let you get in this shape?* First John 5:18 says, "But he that is begotten of God keepeth himself, and that wicked one toucheth him not." My friend, if you are in bad shape, YOU let yourself get there. God has been doing everything He can to get you to simply take His Word for your deliverance and release your faith in the covenant. He is ready to establish His covenant with you in your generation. Walk in the faith of Abraham and you will walk in the blessing of Abraham (Romans 4:16).

Don't let Satan get this far in a temptation and trial. Stop him the first time he moves to challenge your faith. If you have foolishly allowed him to sell you doubt and unbelief, *make yourself act on the Word whether you want to or not.* Get it before your eyes; make your ears listen to God's Word. Get the Word working in your spirit. If outside help is necessary, call a person of faith, but don't continue to cow down in defeat under Satan's dominion when Jesus paid the price for your freedom.

Count It All Joy!

"My brethren, count it all joy when ye fall into divers temptations; knowing this, that the trying of your faith worketh patience. But let patience have her perfect work, that ye may be perfect and entire, wanting nothing" (James 1:2-4).

Count it all joy. Why? Because this is one more opportunity for you to prove that the Word of God works. You have a covenant with God. You have authority over Satan. You have the Name of Jesus and the gifts of the Spirit. He that is within you is greater than he that is in the world. Your weapons are mighty through God to the pulling down of Satan's strongholds. This test and trial will be like the others in which God's Word has brought you victory. You know that when you release your faith, Satan tries to deceive you into changing your words of faith from success to defeat, from health to sickness, and from abundance to poverty. You know who your enemy is, how he tempts you, and what to do about it.

Count it all joy because you know that the trying of your faith worketh (exerciseth) patience. Trials do not cause you to have patience; they cause you to use or work the patience that you have. You have made a decision of your will to stand in faith until the results are seen. The power of patience is at work in your life. *Patience will have her perfect work that you may be perfect and entire, wanting nothing.* You will not be moved off the Word of God. Your patience will not yield to circumstances or succumb to trial. *You should count it all joy!* The results of your prayers are inevitable.

"Blessed is the man that endureth temptation: for when he is tried, he shall receive the crown of life, which the Lord hath promised to them that love him" (James 1:12). When the Bible says *blessed,* it means *blessed!* Every man is not blessed. The blessed man is one who endures temptation without yielding to Satan's pressure to faint and give up what belongs to him in God's Word. The man is blessed who trusts in his covenant with God to provide whatever he needs.

"When he is tried, he shall receive." This man has been tried and found faithful to God's Word. *Satan himself has proven the man's faith.* There is nothing left for that man but to receive what he has asked of God. He receives whatever he has trusted God's Word to obtain. God will establish His covenant in his life. The crown of life is God's very best—not only His best in heaven, but the very best life has to offer on earth. W. E. Vine says that *crown* is used in this instance as *emblem of life, joy, reward and glory.* (Similar uses are found in Philippians 4:1 and 1 Thessalonians 2:19.) The crown of life is life perfected, completed, with finishing touches. We would say "the icing on the cake."

I never before this moment saw that Satan can only hurt his own cause by tempting the believer who refuses to doubt God's Word. Satan's temptation PROVES the steadfast believer's faith. Every time Satan comes at you with temptation, test and trial and you endure that temptation without yielding to his pressure, Satan proves that you believe God. When you passed the test—the trying of your faith—Satan sealed his own defeat in your life.

Satan calls attention to the fact that you believe God and that he could not make you compromise God's Word. Heaven sees that you believe God. The earth sees that you believe God. The angels see that you believe God. The demons see that you believe God and that their leader can do nothing in the face of the Word of God.

When the believer does not yield to Satan's demands, it makes Satan look bad! Satan takes a great risk when he attacks an uncompromising believer. That believer can *either* yield to Satan's pressure or hold fast to his confession of faith in God's Word. The believer who depends on his covenant leaves Satan nothing but defeat.

When you prove to Satan enough times that you will not compromise God's Word, he will stay out of your way. He is a creature of pride. He does not enjoy defeat. He operates his regime on fear. Satan himself is ruled by fear. His defeat makes him look as weak as he really is. He loses face before the cohorts of hell and before the eyes of men. Satan's defeat leaves the believer with the testimony of how he acted on God's Word in the face of adversity and won. In my own opinion and experience, I am convinced that Satan does not bring temptation, test and trial unless he thinks he can win. When you have successfully stood and won over every test he has sent your way for a long while, he is slow to risk the probability of defeat.

"Blessed...is the man whom You discipline and instruct, O Lord, and teach out of Your law, that You may give him power to keep himself calm in the days of adversity, until the [inevitable] pit of corruption is dug for the wicked.... For justice will return to the...righteous, and all the upright in heart will follow it" (Psalm 94:12-13, 15, AMPC).

The Blessed Man

Praise ye the LORD. Blessed is the man that feareth the LORD, that delighteth greatly in his commandments.

His seed shall be mighty upon earth: the generation of the upright shall be blessed.

Wealth and riches shall be in his house: and his righteousness endureth for ever.

Unto the upright there ariseth light in the darkness: he is gracious, and full of compassion, and righteous.

A good man sheweth favour, and lendeth: he will guide his affairs with discretion.

Surely he shall not be moved for ever: the righteous shall be in everlasting remembrance.

He shall not be afraid of evil tidings: his heart is fixed, trusting in the Lord.

His heart is established, he shall not be afraid, until he see his desire upon his enemies.

He hath dispersed, he hath given to the poor; his righteousness endureth for ever; his horn shall be exalted with honour.

The wicked shall see it, and be grieved; he shall gnash with his teeth, and melt away: the desire of the wicked shall perish.

Psalm 112

"Blessed is the man." This man fears the Lord and delights in His Word. He is gracious and full of compassion and righteousness. He shows favor and lends.

He guides his affairs with discretion. He is not moved. "He shall not be afraid of evil tidings: his heart is fixed, trusting in the Lord." This man trusts in the Word of his God. His heart is established in the covenant. He fears no evil.

He has freely distributed and has given to the poor.
He has given and it shall be given to him—good measure,
pressed down, shaken together, and running over.

The Word does not say that his seed possibly would be
mighty upon the earth; it says that his seed *shall* be mighty.
The Word does not say that wealth and riches might be in
his house; it says wealth and riches *shall* be in his house!

"His righteousness endureth for ever; his horn shall be
exalted with honour." Righteousness, riches, and honor
are his to enjoy because he delights in the Word of his God.

Satan will see the blessing of God on this man and be
grieved because he can do nothing to alter God's covenant.
The desire of the wicked shall perish. Satan cannot stop
the blessing of Abraham from being established in this
man's life.

When you are obedient to the Word of God, nothing
can stop wealth and riches from being in your house—
except you. If you will not accept prosperity, God will not
perform beyond what you are willing to receive. But if you
are willing and obedient, you *shall* eat the good of the land!

DEAR PROSPEROUS BELIEVER

Dear Prosperous Believer,

There is no question whatsoever that it is God's perfect will for us to prosper.

By the time he wrote 3 John 2, the Apostle John was called "The Elder." He had become a wise, mature and respected leader in the Church. His integrity was unquestioned. His humility was unparalleled. And his face-to-face relationship with Jesus on the island of Patmos was astounding, to say the least.

That is why this verse is so significant. One listens very closely to a man of great experience, stature and honor in the Body of Christ. Ask me how I know.

"Beloved, I wish above all things that thou mayest prosper and be in health, even as thy soul prospereth." Notice he said "above all things." To see others prosper and be in health was John's overwhelming passion—a passion that came from the Father. Psalm 35:27 says, "Let the Lord be magnified, which hath pleasure in the prosperity of his servant." We also read in Deuteronomy 8:18, "But thou shalt remember the Lord thy God: for it is he that giveth thee power to get wealth, that he may establish his covenant which he sware unto thy fathers, as it is this day." Philippians 4:19 in the *Amplified Bible, Classic Edition*, tells us that "my God will liberally supply (fill to the full) your every need according to His riches in glory in Christ Jesus."

Seeing people prosper is also the passion of Kenneth Copeland Ministries.

I began working for KCM in 1976. I became a student of the solid biblical principles of faith that this ministry teaches. I am quite familiar with its mission, having traveled with Kenneth and Gloria Copeland and by listening to countless messages on cassette tapes and then CDs.

From time to time, Brother Copeland would share with congregations what this ministry is called to do. I would write down what he would say and keep a collection of those "mission statements." One day, he spoke about his calling where prosperity was concerned.

He said, "This ministry is called to teach the laws that govern prosperity and supernatural increase and abundance." I could hear the deep sense of responsibility in his voice. I received that mandate as my own, both as a believer in Christ Jesus and as the pastor of Eagle Mountain International Church.

You can imagine how thrilled and honored I was when, in 2010, Gloria asked me to teach two weeks on the *Believer's Voice of Victory* broadcast. At the time, I was teaching a prosperity series in church.

It was no surprise when the Lord spoke up in my spirit and told me to teach a television series titled "10 Days of Prosperity."

He went on to say, *As much as I want My people healed, I want them to prosper financially and provisionally. I want My people to thrive and flourish in these times. I want them to experience My supernatural provision. Lack and poverty are under the curse. Tell them that they are redeemed from the curse and that they are to walk in the fullness of THE BLESSING. My people are not subject to the times, no matter what is happening around them. Totally immerse them in the Word of prosperity. By doing this, the Word will build their faith and enlarge their capacity to believe and receive. Now, get with the program!* It was a very strong word!

The Lord impressed me to prepare the outlines in advance and make them available to the television audience. I taped the first 10 programs by myself.

Several weeks after the broadcasts aired, I received one of the most significant phone calls of my life. It was Gloria Copeland calling. "George," she said, "I have had a brilliant idea. I just watched your broadcasts and I want you and me to do the next prosperity series. There is one stipulation—I want you to bring your notes!"

I heartily accepted the offer. Those outlines have not been difficult to prepare. I have been taught by the very best! The reference materials are endless. And, what an amazing time we have had. I have learned so much more by taping with Gloria. It is obvious that the message of prosperity is deep within her spirit. I must say that teaching with Gloria has been one of the greatest highlights of my life. What an honor!

I happened to mention something to Gloria while taping our first broadcast together. "Gloria, you just can't exhaust the subject of prosperity," I said. She quickly answered and said, "Let's try!!"

As of the publishing of this 40th anniversary edition, Gloria and I have taped more than 300 prosperity programs. We have included 30 prosperity outlines from those broadcasts. All of our outlines and programs are available on kcm.org.

All of us in the Body of Christ congratulate Gloria Copeland for teaching us that it is truly God's will for us to prosper.

Pastor George Pearsons

Senior Pastor, CEO and
Blessed Son-in-law

21 WAYS
GOD SUPPLIES
191 SCRIPTURES

1. Tithing
- Malachi 3:10
- Leviticus 27:30
- Deuteronomy 26:1-2
- Hebrews 7:8
- Genesis 14:19-20

2. Sowing and Reaping
- Twice-sown seed—John 6:11
- Sowing in famine—Genesis 26:1, 12-14
- These who scatter—Proverbs 11:24-28
- Law of seedtime and harvest—Genesis 8:22; Mark 4:26-32
- Supernatural increase—Psalm 115:12-14
- Deuteronomy 16:15
- 1 Corinthians 3:6
- Psalm 62:10

3. The Law of Multiplication
- Multiplication—Genesis 9:7, 16:10, 17:16; 2 Corinthians 9:10
- Hundredfold return—Mark 4:20, 10:28-30; 2 Samuel 24:3
- One thousand times more—Deuteronomy 1:11; Isaiah 60:22
- Made thee a million—Ezekiel 16:7
- The Double—Isaiah 61:7; Exodus 22:7; Job 42:10

4. Giving to the Poor
- Proverbs 19:17
- Proverbs 28:27
- Psalm 41:1
- Matthew 19:21
- James 2:15-16
- Daniel 4:27
- The poor giving to you—1 Kings 17:9

5. The Ministry
- Giving to the house of the Lord—Haggai 1:7-10; 1 Chronicles 29:17, 25, 28
- Listen to the prophet—2 Chronicles 20:20
- Partnership with ministries—1 Samuel 30:24-25; 2 Kings 4:8-10
- Listen to your pastor—Psalm 23:1; Jeremiah 3:15, 23:3-4
- Increased anointing in hands of ministry—John 6:11-13
- Apostle John's greatest desire—3 John 2
- Prophet's reward—Matthew 10:41
- Righteous man's reward—Matthew 10:41

6. Memorial Giving
- Mark 12:41-44
- Acts 10:4
- Matthew 26:13

7. Our Relationship With God
- Honoring and loving God—Proverbs 3:9-10, 8:17-21
- God's pleasure in us—Psalm 35:27; Luke 12:32
- By seeking Him first—Matthew 6:33-34; Job 22:21
- Being taught by God—Isaiah 48:17

8. Provision Direct From the Throne
- Seed for the sower—2 Corinthians 9:10
- The hand of God—1 Chronicles 29:14-16; Numbers 11:23
- God's own ability for us—Ephesians 3:20; 2 Corinthians 9:8
- Come to the throne—Hebrews 4:16
- Daily provision—Psalm 68:19; Exodus 16:4
- His riches in glory—Philippians 4:19; Ephesians 3:16
- Your heavenly account—Philippians 4:17-20; Matthew 6:19-21
- Wisdom—Proverbs 3:13-15, 4:5-9, 24:3-4

9. By Creation, Re-creation and Restoration
- Creating something from faith—Genesis 1:1;
  Hebrews 11:1-3; Romans 4:17
- Creating something from very little—John 6:11;
  1 Kings 17:13-14; 2 Kings 4:7; Luke 5:5-7
- Re-creation of a substance—John 2:7-10; Luke 3:8
- Supernatural restoration—Joel 2:25; Exodus 22:7;
  Proverbs 6:31

10. Miraculous Provision
- Debt Cancellation—Deuteronomy 15:1-2; Philemon 18-19;
  1 Samuel 17:25, 22:2; 2 Kings 4:7, 6:5-6; Matthew 18:27,
  6:12; Leviticus 25:10; Nehemiah 5:3-4, 11-12
- Reaping where you haven't sown—Leviticus 25:11;
  John 4:38
- Receiving what you didn't ask for—1 Kings 3:13
- Without money—Isaiah 55:1

11. Earth's Resources
- Psalm 24:1
- Psalm 33:5
- Psalm 67:5-6
- Psalm 85:11-12
- Psalm 104:24
- Deuteronomy 32:13
- Genesis 14:19
- Haggai 2:8
- Exodus 19:5
- Psalm 116:16

12. Hidden Treasures of Darkness
- Isaiah 45:3

13. Provision by Individuals
- Men—Luke 6:38; Psalms 68:29, 72:10, 112:5;
  Matthew 7:12; 2 Samuel 23:14-17
- Kings—Proverbs 21:1; Ezra 6:3-4, 7-8; 2 Chronicles 9:12;
  Esther 5:8
- Inheritance from relatives—Proverbs 19:14;
  2 Corinthians 12:14

14. God Uses Us
- The power to get wealth—Deuteronomy 8:18; Proverbs 16:22; Genesis 24:35; Psalm 37:21-22
- Prayer of agreement—Matthew 18:18-20; 2 Kings 7:3, 5-6
- Thanksgiving—Philippians 4:6
- Work—Ephesians 4:28; 2 Thessalonians 3:10; Proverbs 6:6, 10:5, 12:11, 13:11, 14:23, 20:13; Romans 12:11
- Hand of the diligent makes rich—Proverbs 10:14, 12:24
- Thoughts of the diligent—Proverbs 21:5
- Being faithful—Luke 16:10-12, 19:17
- Being generous—1 Timothy 6:17-19
- Developing an established heart—Psalm 112:5-8
- Fasting—Matthew 6:17-18; Isaiah 58:6-8
- Confession—Proverbs 10:20, 12:18, 15:4, 18:21

15. Witty Inventions
- Proverbs 8:12

16. Simply the World's System
- The wicked and the sinner—Proverbs 13:22; Ecclesiastes 2:26; James 5:1-3
- Stolen goods returned—Exodus 22:1; Psalm 79:12; Proverbs 6:30-31, 22:22-23
- Steal it back from the enemy—Exodus 3:21-22, 12:36; 2 Chronicles 20:25; 2 Kings 7:8; Joshua 12:1, 13:1; Isaiah 53:12; 1 Samuel 30:19
- Other nations—Isaiah 61:5, 60:5

17. Angels
- Psalm 103:20-21
- Hebrews 1:14
- 2 Kings 6:17

18. Wildlife
A man shared several years ago of how he spoke to the birds to bring him money. Based upon 1 Kings 17, he said he started finding money outside around the house after he went out and hollered at the birds. They gathered around and listened to him. "People lose money every day. Go get it!"

A 15-year-old was so impressed with this story, he decided to try it. He asked the Lord for $10 for missions and God provided seed to the sower.

He went out and spoke to the birds, commanding them to put it in a tree in the backyard:

Day 1 $1.65
Day 2 $2.35
Day 3 $7
Day 4 $10

Over the next two months, he found $440 in the tree.

- 1 Kings 17:4-6
- Matthew 17:27
- Genesis 22:13-14
- Psalm 50:10

19. Because the Lord Needs It
- Mark 14:13-16
- Mark 11:2-3

20. Our Covenant Inheritance
- The Blessing of Abraham—Galatians 3:13-14
- The righteous will never beg for bread—Psalm 37:25
- Through faith and patience—Hebrews 6:12; James 1:3-5
- Our prosperous lineage—Genesis 17:1-3
- Inheritance through being a joint heir with Jesus—Galatians 3:29; Ephesians 1:10-11; Romans 8:16-17; Psalm 37:18

21. The Favor of God
- Exodus 11:3
- Deuteronomy 33:23
- Joshua 11:20
- 1 Samuel 16:22
- Esther 2:17
- Esther 5:8
- Esther 8:5

DAYS OF PROSPERITY

BY GLORIA COPELAND & PASTOR GEORGE PEARSONS

THRIVING IN THE MIDST OF FAMINE
DAY #4

A. **Genesis 26:1—There Was a Famine in the Land**
   1. *Famine*
      a. Severe shortage
      b. Extreme scarcity
      c. Serious economic downturn
   2. Dark time for those who…
      a. Don't know God
      b. Don't know their covenant with God
      c. Fear, panic, uncertainty, hopelessness
   3. What the Word tells *us* about famine
      a. Job 5:20, 22 (NLT): "He will save you from death in time of famine…. You will laugh at destruction and famine."
      b. Psalm 33:18-19: "The eye of the Lord is upon them that fear him, upon them that hope in His mercy [NLT—rely on His unfailing love]; to deliver their soul from death, and to keep them alive in famine."

      c. Psalm 37:18-19: Even in famine they will have more than enough.
        i. HEB: "...He will supply until no more is needed."
  4. In famine, we don't just survive—<u>WE THRIVE!</u>
      a. Prosper, flourish, succeed, advance
      b. Grow vigorously
      c. Increase in goods and estate
  5. Proverbs 10:22: "The blessing of the Lord, it maketh rich, and he addeth no sorrow with it."

B. **Genesis 26—Isaac Thrived in Famine**
  1. Verses 1-6: Stay where you are—*obedience*.
      a. God needed him there.
      b. God needs us right here, right now.
      c. Zechariah 8:13 (NLT): "Among the other nations, Judah and Israel became symbols of a cursed nation. But no longer! Now, I will rescue you and *make you both a symbol and a source of blessing*. So don't be afraid. Be strong, and get on with rebuilding the temple!"
      d. We are a symbol of THE BLESSING
      e. We are a source of THE BLESSING
        i. Genesis 12:2-3 (AMPC): "I will make of you a great nation, and I will bless you [with abundant increase of favors] and make your name famous and distinguished, and you will be a blessing [dispensing good to others].... In you will all the families and kindred of the earth be blessed [and by you they will bless themselves]."
        ii. Psalm 21:6 (AMPC): "...You make him to be blessed and a blessing forever."
  2. Verse 12: He sowed and received *in the same year* one hundredfold—and the Lord blessed him.
      a. *Unusual yield*—even in fertile regions, not greater than twenty-five to fiftyfold

    b. Psalm 65:11-13 (NLT): "You crown the year with a bountiful harvest; even the hard pathways overflow with abundance. The grasslands of the wilderness become a lush pasture, and the hillsides blossom with joy. The meadows are clothed with flocks of sheep, and the valleys are carpeted with grain. They all shout and sing for joy!"

    c. In the same year

3. Verse 13: Isaac waxed great, went forward and became very great.

    a. (NLT): He became a rich man and his wealth only continued to grow.

    b. He was thriving—flourishing, succeeding, advancing, growing vigorously, increasing in goods, estates, bulk and stature.

    c. He became stronger and more powerful in wealth and influence.

4. Verse 14: He had possessions of flocks of sheep, herds of cattle and a great store of servants.

    a. Philistines were jealous.

    b. They wanted to stop him.

5. Verses 22-24: He didn't give up—he wouldn't quit.

    a. *Rehobeth* (HEB) = room, streets, a broad and spacious place, an enlargement.

    b. (NLT): "…At last the Lord has created enough space for us to prosper [thrive, flourish, succeed, advance and grow vigorously] in this land."

C. In Order to Thrive in Times of Famine, We Must Keep Doing What Isaac Did

1. Keep obeying God.

    a. Obedience is where THE BLESSING is

    b. Isaiah 1:19: "If ye be willing and obedient, ye shall eat the good of the land."

2. Keep sowing seed.

    a. It is always a good time to sow into the kingdom of God

  b. Ecclesiastes 11:4 (AMPC): "He who observes the wind [and waits for all conditions to be favorable] will not sow, and he who regards the clouds will not reap."

3. Keep tithing.

  a. Isaac tithed—how do we know?

  b. Genesis 14:20: Abraham gave tithes of all.

  c. Genesis 18:19: "For I know him, that he will command his children and his household after him, and they shall keep the way of the Lord…."

4. Keep on walking by faith.

  a. Isaac didn't quit standing in faith.

  b. Hebrews 10:35 (AMPC): "Do not, therefore, fling away your fearless confidence, for it carries a great and glorious compensation of reward."

  c. Galatians 6:9 (AMPC): "Let us not lose heart and grow weary and faint in acting nobly and doing right, for in due time and at the appointed season we shall reap, if we do not loosen and relax our courage and faint."

5. Psalm 92:12-14: Keep attending church.

  a. Verse 12: "The righteous shall flourish like the palm tree: he shall grow like a cedar in Lebanon."

  b. Verse 13: "Those that be planted in the house of the Lord shall flourish in the courts of our God."

  c. Verse 14: "They shall still bring forth fruit in old age; they shall be fat and flourishing."

    i. Our future is secure in Him.

D. Thriving In a Time of Famine—Confession

I am not moved by what I see.
I am not moved by what I hear.
I am going up higher.
I am going to keep obeying.

I am going to keep sowing.
I am going to keep believing.
I am going to keep receiving.
I am going to keep on walking by faith.
In a time of famine, we are thriving.
We are prospering.
We are flourishing.
We are succeeding.
We are advancing.
We are growing vigorously.
We are increasing.

WALKING IN THE FULLNESS
OF THE BLESSING
DAY #5

A. **Romans 15:29—The Fullness of The Blessing**
1. (GNB): I shall come with a full measure of The Blessing.
2. *Fullness* = Greek word *pleroma*
3. To be filled up, full, complete, to be fully furnished and liberally supplied
   a. Philippians 4:19 (AMPC) "My God will liberally supply (fill to the full) your every need according to His riches in glory in Christ Jesus."
4. To fill to the top so that nothing is wanting; to fill to the brim so that nothing is lacking
   a. Example of a ship fully manned with sailors, rowers and soldiers and fully loaded with supplies, freight and merchandise
5. *Plethora*—overabundance, excessive amount, superabundance

B. **Genesis 1:27-28—A Quick Review of The Blessing**
1. The very first words heard by a human ear, setting the course and precedent for God's perfect will for man
2. Man was empowered by The Blessing in order to:
   a. Be fruitful
   b. Multiply
   c. Replenish the earth
   d. Subdue the earth
   e. Have dominion over the earth
3. The Garden of Eden was a perfect demonstration of God's plan for this planet. It was a prototype of what He wanted the planet to look like. Adam's job was to exercise his God-given authority and expand that Garden until it encompassed the entire earth. That was what The Blessing was for.

4. It provided Adam with the power to carry on the work God began at Creation. It equipped him with the divine resources he needed to follow God's example. He was to transform the uncultivated parts of this planet into a veritable Garden of Eden by speaking faith-filled words. The Blessing empowered Adam to be The Blessing wherever he went. The Garden of Eden was literally inside Adam.

5. Jesus came to restore The Blessing that was lost at the Fall
   a. Jesus is The Blessing—the last Adam.
   b. Jesus—The Blessing—now is alive in us.
   c. We have been redeemed from the curse and now walk in The Blessing of Abraham.

C. Galatians 3:13-14—Redeemed From the Curse to Walk in The Blessing

1. *Redeem*—to buy back, to buy out, to clear by payment
2. To free a person from captivity by paying a ransom
3. We have been freed from the curse of poverty.
   a. Lack
   b. Deficiency
   c. Not enough
   d. Shortage
4. We are redeemed from "paycheck-to-paycheck," just barely getting along.
5. Proverbs 10:22: "The blessing of the Lord, it maketh rich, and He addeth no sorrow with it."

D. Deuteronomy 28:1-14—Walking in the Fullness of The Blessing

1. Verse 2: All these blessings shall come on you and overtake you.
   a. Brenton: All these blessings shall come upon you and shall find you
   b. HEB = will reach you
2. Verse 8 (MSG): "God will order a blessing on your barns and workplaces...."

     a. CEV: "The Lord your God is giving you the land, and He will make sure you are successful in everything you do...."
3. Verse 11 (MSG): "God will lavish you with good things...."
     a. AMPC: "The Lord shall make you have a surplus of prosperity...."
     b. BBE: "The Lord will make you fertile in every good thing...."
     c. NRSV: "The Lord will make you abound in prosperity...."
4. Verse 12 (MSG): "God will throw open the doors of His sky vaults and pour rain on your land on schedule and bless the work you take in hand. You will lend to many nations but you yourself won't have to take out a loan."
     a. AMPC: "The Lord shall open to you His good treasury...."
     b. NLT: "The Lord will send rain at the proper time from His rich treasury in the heavens and will bless the work you do...."
     c. *Treasury* in the Hebrew = depository, armory
     d. BBE: He will open His storehouse in heaven.
     e. CEV: "The Lord will open the storehouses of the skies."
5. I am walking in the fullness of The Blessing, fully furnished and liberally supplied.
Filled to the top—nothing wanting.
Filled to the brim—nothing lacking.
My ship is full and overflowing.
The Blessing has come to me.
The Blessing has overtaken me.
I am walking in the superabundant, exceeding excess, fullness of The Blessing.

Our Relationship to Money
DAY #6

A. The Role of Money in Our Lives
1. Money issues can be a source of stress and pressure.
2. They control lives, attitudes and emotions.
3. Some are slaves to money—driven to make it and keep it.
4. We must straighten out our relationship with money.
5. Goal: Financial Attitude Adjustment

B. Matthew 6:24-33—Settle This: I Serve God. Money Serves Me.
1. Genesis 1:29: Seed was designed by God to serve us.
2. Psalm 104:14: Seed is for the service of man.
3. Mark 10:17-22: Example of a man serving money.
4. Mark 12:41-44: Example of money serving a woman.
    a. 2 Corinthians 9:6: This is what she did.

C. 1 Timothy 6:10, 17-19: How We Conduct Ourselves With Money
1. Verse 10: The love of money is the root of all evil.
2. We don't love money—we love God.
3. Verse 17: We don't trust money—we trust God.
4. Verse 18: We are givers of money—not takers.
5. Money is a tool to help others.

D. My Confession of Faith

I settle this issue right now.
I adjust my financial attitude.

I do not serve money.
I am not a slave to money.
I serve God.
Money serves me.

I do not work for money.
Money works for me.
Money doesn't control me—I control money.
Money doesn't rule me—I rule money.
Money doesn't dominate me—I dominate money.

I fearlessly tithe as I am told.
I boldly give as I am led.
Money—you serve me.
Money—you obey me.
Money—you multiply, increase and produce maximum harvest.

Harvest—I command you to come to me now—in Jesus' Name!

SUPERNATURAL PROVISION
DAY #7

A. **Matthew 17:24-27—Money in a Fish's Mouth**
   1. Demonstration of supernatural provision—"Bring it on, birds!" Testimony Tommy Williams shared several years ago how he spoke to the birds to bring him money. Based upon 1 Kings 17, Tommy started finding money around the house after he went out and hollered at the birds.

   A 15-year-old was so impressed with this story that he decided to try it. He asked the Lord for $10 for missions.

   He went out, spoke to the birds and commanded them to put it in a tree in the backyard. The first day he discovered 65 cents, the second day $2.35, and the third day $7. Over the next two months, he found a total of $440 in the tree!
   2. Foreign to natural man's thinking
   3. Unusual, unlimited, accelerated supply from heaven
   4. Supersedes the realm of impossibility
   5. God has supernatural ways to fully supply every need in the face of lack, shortage and a bad economy.
      a. He makes the way when they say there is no way.

B. **What We Must Do to Experience Supernatural Provision**
   1. Enlarge our capacity for supernatural provision
   2. See God supernaturally supplying the need
   3. Feed on the Word
   4. Renew our minds
   5. Exercise our faith

C. **Faith-Building Scriptures for Supernatural Provision**
   1. James 1:17: "Every good gift and every perfect gift [AMPC—free, large, full] is from above, and cometh down from the Father of lights, with whom is no

variableness, neither shadow of turning.
2. Ephesians 3:20-21 (AMPC): "Now to Him Who, by
the [action of His] power that is at work within us,
is able to [carry out His purpose and] do superabun-
dantly, far over and above all that we [dare] ask or
think [infinitely beyond our highest prayers, desires,
thoughts, hopes or dreams]—to Him be glory in the
church...."
3. Philippians 4:19 (AMPC): "My God will liberally
supply (fill to the full) your every need according to
His riches in glory in Christ Jesus."
a. *Supply* in the Greek—fill up, make full, furnish
liberally, fill to the top so that nothing shall be
wanting, fill to the brim so that nothing shall be
lacking
4. Psalm 68:19: "Blessed be the Lord, who daily loads us
with benefits, even the God of our salvation."
5. Isaiah 55:1: "Every one that thirsteth, come to the
waters, and he that hath no money; come ye, buy, and
eat; yea, come, buy wine and milk without money and
without price."

D. Examples of Supernatural Provision
1. Genesis 22:6-14: God supernaturally provided a ram
for the sacrifice.
a. Verse 14: Abraham called the name of that
place, "The Lord will provide."
2. 1 Kings 17:1-6: God supernaturally provided ravens to
bring food and drink to Elijah.
3. 1 Kings 17:8-16: God supernaturally provided a one-
year supply of food for the widow in the midst of a
famine.
a. Verse 14: The barrel of meal and the bottle of
oil would not be empty until the rain returned.
b. Verse 15: She, he and her house did eat a full
year.
c. Verse 16 (NLT): No matter how much they
used, there was always enough left over in the

containers.
4. 2 Kings 4:1-7: God supernaturally provided supernatural debt cancellation for the widow.
   a. The woman kept pouring oil from a small pot into as many empty vessels as they could find.
5. 2 Kings 6:1-7: God supernaturally caused a borrowed, lost ax head to float to the surface of the water.
6. John 2:1-11: Jesus supernaturally turned water into wine.
   a. 180 gallons of wine
7. John 6:5-14: Jesus supernaturally multiplies the fish and loaves and feeds 20,000.
   a. Word from the Lord through Brother Copeland, "You are going to be the ones who God uses to supernaturally feed the lost when disasters come. Only, it is not going to be like it was in the past. In many cases, you are not even going to need the trucks and airplanes. In a lot of cases, you are just going to take one little meal and divide it and divide it and divide it."
   b. Jesus touched the loaves and fishes and they supernaturally multiplied.

E. **Galatians 6:7-8—Sowing Is a Supernatural Action**
   1. "Those who give shall walk in the ways of the supernatural." —Kenneth Copeland
   2. When you sow into the kingdom of God, you reap from the kingdom of God.
   3. Giving and tithing are supernatural acts.
   4. Expect to reap supernatural things.
   5. There are many supernatural streams of provision and income available in God's kingdom—believe and receive!

SUPERNATURAL DEBT CANCELLATION
DAY #8

A. **Luke 4:14-21—Three Ways God Supernaturally Removes Debt**
   1. He provides the finances.
   2. He removes the debt.
   3. He moves upon others.

B. **He Provides the Finances**
   1. 2 Kings 4:1-7 (NLT): "...Sell the olive oil and pay your debts, and you and your sons can live on what is left over."
   2. Luke 5:1-11: Simon Peter's fishing business avoided bankruptcy after Jesus told him where to drop the nets.
   3. Matthew 17:24-27: Taxes were paid from money in a fish's mouth.

C. **He Removes the Debt**
   1. Nehemiah 5:1-13: Nehemiah cancelled the debts of the poor Jews.
   2. Matthew 18:23-27: The king forgave his servant of the 10,000 talents.
   3. Matthew 6:12: Key point—forgive us our debts as we forgive our debtors.
   4. Colossians 2:13-14 (AMPC): Jesus "cancelled and blotted out and wiped away the handwriting of the note...with its legal decrees and demands. He set it aside and cleared it completely out of our way by nailing it to [His] cross."
   5. Luke 16:1-7: He reduces the debt.
      a. EMIC testimony—debt reduced 75 percent (from $6,500 down to $1,600)

D. **He Moves Upon Others**
   1. Philemon 18-19 (AMPC): "If he has done you any wrong in any way, or owes anything [to you], charge

that to my account. I, Paul, write it with my own hand—I promise to pay it in full...."

2. Luke 10:30-37: The Samaritan took out two pence and gave them to the owner of the inn and said to him, "Take care of him. Whatever else you have to spend, I will pay it back in full when I return."

3. God is the One who moves upon a person—not you.
   a. Faith puts no pressure on others.
   b. Faith puts pressure on the Word of the covenant.
   c. Faith says, "God is my source."
   d. Luke 6:38: You give and it will be given to you.

E. Word From the Lord Through Brother Copeland

1. The manifestation of The Blessing is at an all-time high. You are approaching a "Blessing manifestation of glory" that is an explosion in ways and intensity that the human race has never seen before.

2. The Blessing will surround you. The Blessing will incase you. You will learn to walk in the secret place of the Most High God, blessed in His Blessing, blessed in His glory, blessed in your comings, blessed in your goings and blessed in your pocketbook.

3. All debt will have to get up and leave you the way leprosy left the lepers of old.

4. Debt is financial sickness. It is financial leprosy. It is an attempt to do with the natural world's monies and abilities what I created The Blessing to do for you. Only, it is a burden and not a blessing. Debt is part of the curse.

5. If you will begin to confess the Word, you will be shocked and thrilled at how quickly you will have the glory arise and drive the debt out of your life.

6. If you will bring your tithe to Me and spend time with Me, tithing that tithe to Me, I will teach you and I will train you and I will show you how to be debt free. I will bless you beyond your means. I will bless you beyond your income. I will bless you beyond your salaries. I will bless you beyond anything you have ever

known before. I will show you things that you have never heard of before.

7. You will take advantage of those things and be financially blessed. I will bring such a financial blessing upon you that you won't have any idea where it came from. It has come to an explosive place.

8. I am ready, saith the Lord, if you will begin to confess it, walk in it and make it a priority in your life. Then, the glory will manifest in the midst and you will give Me praise. I will come and visit you and together, we will have a grand time.

MAKING WITHDRAWALS FROM
OUR HEAVENLY ACCOUNT
DAY #9

A. Philippians 4:14-19—The Bank of Heaven
1. There are bank accounts on earth.
   a. Philemon 18 (AMPC): "If he has done you any wrong in any way or owes anything [to you], charge that to my account."
   b. John 12:6 (AMPC): Judas had the "bag, the money box, the purse of the Twelve."
   c. 2 Chronicles 31:11: Hezekiah commanded [the people] to prepare chambers [in the Hebrew, *storehouses*] in the house of the Lord.
   d. You can have earthly accounts—just don't put your trust in them.
2. There are bank accounts in heaven.
   a. Matthew 6:19-21: They are not subject to theft, ruin, corruption or economic conditions of any kind.
   b. Luke 12:33—A treasure in heaven that fails not.
3. Many do not realize they already have an account in heaven.
4. The Philippians had established an account in heaven.
   a. Verse 15 (GOS): "No church but yours went into partnership and opened an account with us."
   b. They opened their account by giving.
5. Verse 17 (AMPC): Not that I seek or am eager for [your] gift, but I do seek and am eager for the fruit which increases to your credit [the harvest of blessing that is accumulating to your account]."
   a. CON: I seek fruit which accrues to your account.
   b. TCNT: I am anxious to see abundant returns placed to your account.
   c. MOFFAT: I am anxious for the interest that accumulates to your divine account.

d.   NASB: I seek for the profit which increases to
     your account.
e.   NJB: What I value most is the interest that is
     mounting up in your account.

B.   Matthew 6:19-21—Making Deposits
1.   *Lay up*—make deposits
2.   Malachi 3:10: Tithing
3.   Mark 10:29-30: Investing in the gospel
4.   Proverbs 19:17: Giving to the poor
     a.   Matthew 19:21: "Go and sell that thou hast,
          and give to the poor, and thou shalt have trea-
          sure in heaven."
5.   1 Chronicles 16:29: Giving as a praise to God

C.   1 Timothy 6:17-19—Making Withdrawals
Kenneth and Gloria Copeland were living in Tulsa,
Okla. He was a preacher without a place to preach and
driving a worn-out car with 95,000 "hard" miles. They had
children to take care of and college to pay for. Up until
this point, their financial track record was not good at all.

They owed people with no apparent way to ever pay
them back.

But after hearing Kenneth E. Hagin preach about
faith from Mark 11:23, they decided to take action. They
gathered all their debts. They listed every person and
the amount owed. They calculated in great detail what
it would take for them to operate their household. They
included a 15% pad in their budget for extras. They determined what they needed in their immediate future. All of
this information was written on paper in a formal prayer of
agreement.

Days went by before they would sign their names to
the agreement. They prayed and fasted. They repented
before God for not being a good representative of the Lord
Jesus Christ. They agreed together according to Romans
13:8 that they would never borrow another dime. They
committed to God that they would pay back everyone they

owed. They continued to make deposits into their heavenly account by faithfully tithing and sowing seed.

They released their faith and made a withdrawal from their heavenly bank account.

This process took time, effort, prayer, focus and diligence. They saturated themselves with God's Word and cut off every voice of the world—no TV or newspapers—just the Word of God.

Praise God—twelve months from that day, every debt was paid in full and every need was completely met.

D. **Seven-Point Bank of Heaven Withdrawal**
1. Decide on the amount you need (James 1:5-8).
    a. Be exact and single-minded.
    b. Write it down.
    c. List your needs, debts and desires.
2. Get in agreement with people of like faith (Matthew 18:19-20).
3. Claim what you need by faith (Mark 11:23-24).
4. Bind the devil and his forces (Matthew 18:18).
    a. "Satan, take your hands off my money!"
5. Loose the angels to go get it (Hebrews 1:4).
    a. "Ministering spirits—go get my money!"
6. Continually praise God for it (Psalm 34:1).
7. Avoid strife and unforgiveness (James 3:16; Mark 11:25-26).

E. **Sample Prayer of Agreement**
"Father, in the Name of Jesus, we make a withdrawal of $_____ from our heavenly bank account. We have this money in our account and we are withdrawing this amount now. We believe we receive $_____. As in Mark 11:23-24, we believe it in our hearts and confess now that it is ours in the Name of Jesus. We agree that we have this amount according to Matthew 18:19. From this day forward, we roll the care of this over on to You and thank You for it. Satan, we take authority over you; we bind your operation now and render you helpless. Ministering spirits, we charge you to go forth and cause this amount to come

to us according to Hebrews 1:14. Father, we praise Your Name for meeting our needs according to Your riches in glory by Christ Jesus, and for multiplying our seed for sowing, in the Name of Jesus."

Call In Your Harvest
DAY #10

A. Word From Keith Moore to EMIC About Harvesting—9/28/99

1. Concerning EMIC's giving, God's heart is grieved. It is bothering God that we are not reaping. People are deceived in their thinking if they are just waiting on God to bring it to them.
2. Some are disillusioned and aggravated with God. "How much more can I give?" You think you are waiting on God. You think reaping is automatic. You think once you put the money in, it's all up to Him. You just sit back and relax and think it's all going to just come on you. That is ignorance and confusion.
3. I challenge you to hear the word of the Lord and make up your mind. "I am not just a good giver. I am a good reaper. I am going to get real good at reaping."
4. Proverbs 10: 4-5: "He becometh poor that dealeth with a slack hand: but the hand of the diligent maketh rich. He that gathereth in summer is a wise son: but he that sleepeth in harvest is a son that causeth shame."
5. We can't sleep through our harvest or allow our harvest to stand in the field.

B. Mark 4:26-29—Harvesting Is Our Responsibility

1. The man did the sowing, God gave the increase and the man did the reaping.
2. Proverbs 6:6-8: "Go to the ant, thou sluggard; consider her ways, and be wise: which having no guide, overseer, or ruler, provideth her meat in the summer, and gathereth her food in the harvest."
3. Ecclesiastes 11:4: "He that observeth the wind shall not sow; and he that regardeth the clouds shall not reap."
4. Galatians 6:7-9: "Be not deceived; God is not mocked; for whatsoever a man soweth, that shall he also reap.

For he that soweth to his flesh shall of the flesh reap corruption; but he that soweth to the Spirit shall of the Spirit reap life everlasting. And let us not be weary in well doing: for in due season we shall reap, if we faint not."

5. Ecclesiastes 3:1-2 (NLT): "For everything there is a season, a time for every activity under heaven. A time to be born and a time to die. A time to plant and a time to harvest."

C. How to Reap Your Harvest

1. A preacher was struggling financially. Physically, he was well and strong. He had powerful demonstrations of the spirit. The ministry was growing. The only area of trouble was in the financial realm. He took time to fast and pray, seeking the Lord to find out why. The Lord told him that he was not in faith where his finances were concerned. He told him that he had to receive his finances the same way he received his healing—by faith.
2. We call in our harvest by faith.
3. Isaiah 41:15: "I will make thee a new sharp threshing instrument having teeth...."
   a. *Teeth* in the Hebrew = mouths
   b. Mouths harvest whatever they speak.
4. Our words of faith bring in the harvest.
5. Command the angels to go get our harvest.
   a. Hebrews 1:14: "Are they not all ministering spirits, sent forth to minister for them who shall be heirs of salvation?"
   b. Matthew 13:39: The reapers are the angels.
   c. Psalm 103:20: "Bless the Lord, ye his angels, that excel in strength, that do His commandments, harkening unto the voice of his word."

NOT SUBJECT TO THE TIMES
DAY #11

A. We Are Not Subject to the Times

1. We are not subject to, nor do we live under, the dominion, rule, control or influence of whichever way the economy and the world system are going at the moment.

2. Our times are subject to the authority of the Word, the blood and the Name of Jesus spoken and acted upon by the believer.

3. The times are subject to us.

4. We are subject to and governed by another economy and another system—the kingdom of God.

5. We live in the secret place.
   a. Psalm 27:1-6: "In the time of trouble he shall hide me in his pavilion...."
   b. Psalm 32:6-7: "Thou art my hiding place...."
   c. Psalm 31:14-15: "My times are in thy hand...."

B. John 17:13-22—We Are Separated From the World's Failing System

1. We are to thrive and not just survive.
   a. *Survive*—barely get by, merely exist
   b. *Thrive*—flourish, succeed, advance, prosper

2. Verse 14: We are not of this world's system.

3. Verse 15: "...Keep them from the evil."
   a. Matthew 6:13: "Deliver us from evil...."
   b. Galatians 1:4: "...Deliver us from this present evil world."
   c. 1 John 5:18: "...That wicked one toucheth him not."
   d. 1 Corinthians 10:13: God has made a way to escape.

4. Verse 17: Sanctified from the world through the Word
   a. *Sanctified*—separated and cut away from the effects of

      b. Romans 8:2: "The law of the Spirit of life in Christ Jesus hath made me free [has separated me] from the law of sin and death."

5. We thrive and prosper in tough times.
    a. We are not subject to the economy.
    b. We flourish in spite of what is happening.
    c. Untouched and unaffected

C. Exodus 8:23—The Wall of Redemption

1. Verses 20-23: No swarms of flies
2. 9:1-7: Cattle didn't die
3. 9:22-26: No hail
4. 10:21-23: No darkness in the land
5. Galatians 3:13: Separated from the curse
    a. Verse 9: "They which be of faith are blessed...."

D. Jeremiah 17:5-8—Same Conditions, Different Results

1. The cursed man trusts himself, his heart is not toward God.
2. The result: no fruit, no hope, no future
3. The blessed man trusts God with his whole heart.
4. The result: thriving tree, roots deep, no fear, produces fruit
5. Verse 8 (MSG): "They're like trees replanted in Eden, putting down roots near the rivers—never a worry through the hottest of summers, never dropping a leaf, serene and calm through droughts, bearing fresh fruit every season."

E. Genesis 26:1—Isaac Sowed in Famine and Reaped a Hundredfold

Supernatural Wealth Transfer
DAY #13

A. Financial Inversion Shall Increase in These Days
Word from the Lord through Charles Capps,
February 1, 1978

Financial inversion shall increase in these days. For you see, it is My desire to move in the realm of your financial prosperity. But release Me, saith the Lord, release Me that I may come in your behalf and move on your behalf.

For yes, yes, yes, there shall be in this hour financial distress here and there. The economy shall go up and it will go down; but those who learn to walk in the Word, they shall see the prosperity of the Word come forth in this hour in a way that has not been seen by men in days past.

Yes, there's coming a financial inversion in the world's system. It's been held in reservoirs of wicked men for days on end. But the end is nigh. Those reservoirs shall be tapped and shall be drained into the gospel of Jesus Christ. It shall be done, saith the Lord. It shall be done in the time allotted and so shall it be that the Word of the Lord shall come to pass that the wealth of the sinner is laid up for the just.

Predominantly in two ways shall it be done in this hour. Those who have hoarded up and stored because of the inspiration of the evil one and held the money from the gospel shall be converted and drawn into the kingdom. But many, many will not. They'll not heed the voice of the Word of God. They'll turn aside to this and they'll turn to that and they'll walk in their own ways, but their ways will not work in this hour. It'll dwindle and it'll slip away as though it were in bags with holes in them. It'll go here and it'll go there and they'll wonder why it's not working now. "It worked in days past," they'll say.

But it shall be, saith the Lord, that the Word of the Lord shall rise within men—men of God of low esteem in the financial world—who shall claim the Word of God to be their very own and walk in the light of it as it has been set forth in the Word, and give. They'll begin to give small at first because that's all they have, but then it will increase, and through the hundredfold return, so shall it be that the reservoirs that have held the riches in days past, so shall it return to the hands of the giver. Because of the hundredfold return shall the reservoirs be lost from the wicked and turned to the gospel. For it shall be, it shall be in this hour that you will see things that you've never dreamed come to pass. Oh, it'll be strong at first in ways, then it will grow greater and greater until men will be astounded and the world will stand in awe because the ways of men have failed and the ways of God shall come forth.

As men walk in My Word, so shall they walk in the ways of the Lord. Oh yes, there will be some who say, "Yes, but God's ways are higher, surely higher than our ways, and we can't walk in those." It's true that the ways of God are higher. They are higher than your ways as the heavens are above the earth, but I'll teach you to walk in My ways. I never did say you couldn't walk in My ways. Now learn to walk in them. Learn to give. So shall the inversion of the financial system revert and so shall it be that the gospel of the kingdom shall be preached to all the world, and there shall be no lack in the kingdom. Those who give shall walk in the ways of the supernatural! They shall be known abroad. My Word shall spread and the knowledge of the Lord shall fill all the earth in the day and the hour in which ye stand. Ye shall see it and know it, for it is of Me, and it shall come to pass, saith the Lord.

B. **Proverbs 13:22—The Wealth of the Sinner Is Laid Up for the Just**
    1. AMPC: "…The wealth of the sinner [finds its way eventually] into the hands of the righteous, for whom it was laid up."

C. **Job 27:16-17 (NIV):** "Though he heaps up silver like dust and clothes like piles of clay, what he lays up the righteous will wear, and the innocent will divide his silver."

1. NLT: "Evil people may have piles of money and may store away mounds of clothing. But the righteous will wear that clothing, and the innocent will divide that money."
2. Verse 19 (NLT): "The wicked go to bed rich but wake to find that all their wealth is gone."

D. **Ecclesiastes 2:26 (NIV):** "To the person who pleases him, God gives wisdom, knowledge and happiness, but to the sinner he gives the task of gathering and storing up wealth to hand it over to the one who pleases God...."
   1. NLT: "...If a sinner becomes wealthy, God takes the wealth away and gives it to those who please Him."

E. **Proverbs 28:8 (NLT):** "Income from charging high interest rates will end up in the pocket of someone who is kind to the poor."

F. **Psalm 105:37 (AMPC):** "He brought [Israel] forth also with silver and gold, and there was not one feeble person among their tribes."
   1. *Feeble* (Hebrew) = there was not one pauper among their tribes.
   2. *Pauper*
      a. An extremely poor person
      b. A person without any means of support
      c. A destitute person who depends on aid from public welfare funds or charity
   3. *Tehillim* Commentary
      a. Rabbi Eliezer the Great taught: The lowliest among the children of Israel brought ninety donkeys laden with silver and gold when he left Egypt.
      b. The pauper is a man who has become impoverished and stumbled from his original financial level. No Jew who left Egypt could be described as a pauper because all were enriched by the

possessions of their oppressors.

c. Ibn Yachya and Sforno describe the pauper as a man whose health has deteriorated to the point that he stumbles unless he uses a cane. When the Jews left Egypt, a miracle occurred— not a single person among them was sick or debilitated.

G. Psalm 105:43 (AMPC): "He brought forth his people with joy, and his chosen ones with gladness and singing."

    1. *Tehillim* Commentary

        a. God did not merely load their saddlebags with material wealth.

        b. He filled their hearts with spiritual wealth.

        c. The redeemed ones reaped a rich harvest of faith, the outgrowth of the wonders they beheld.

        d. This filled their hearts with mirth and their mouths with song.

Jehovah Jireh—
Our Supernatural Provider
DAY #15

Our God has unlimited avenues and unusual ways of providing that extend beyond our natural limitations.

A. **Genesis 22:1-14:** Jehovah Jireh—the Lord will provide
    1. Verse 14: "And Abraham called the name of that place Jehovah-jireh: as it is said to this day, In the mount of the Lord it shall be seen."
    2. Verse 14 (CEV): "Abraham named that place, 'The Lord Will Provide.' And even now people say, 'On the mountain of the Lord it will be provided.'"

B. **Leviticus 26:4-5, 9-10 (AMPC):** "I will give you rain in due season, and the land shall yield her increase and the trees of the field yield their fruit. And your threshing [time] shall reach to the vintage and the vintage [time] shall reach to the sowing time, and you shall eat your bread to the full and dwell in your land securely. ...For I will be leaning toward you with favor and regard for you, rendering you fruitful, multiplying you, and establishing and ratifying My covenant with you. And you shall eat the [abundant] old store of produce long kept, and clear out the old [to make room] for the new."
    1. Verse 10 (NLT): "You will have such a surplus of crops that you will need to get rid of the leftovers from the previous year to make room for each new harvest."
    2. Verse 10 (NIV): "You will still be eating last year's harvest when you will have to move it out to make room for the new."

C.   **Deuteronomy 28:8, 11-12 (AMPC):** "The Lord shall command the blessing upon you in your storehouse and in all that you undertake. And He will bless you in the land which the Lord your God gives you. ...And the Lord shall make you have surplus of prosperity, through the fruit of your body, of your livestock, and of your ground, in the land which the Lord swore to your fathers to give you. The Lord shall open to you His good treasury, the heavens to give the rain of your land in its season and to bless all the work of your hands; and you shall lend to many nations, but you shall not borrow."

D.   **1 Samuel 2:8 (AMPC):** "He raises up the poor out of the dust and lifts up the needy from the ash heap [NLT—garbage dump], to make them sit with nobles and inherit the throne of glory. For the pillars of the earth are the Lord's, and He has set the world upon them."

   1.   *The glory of God*—the presence of God heavy with everything good

E.   **Psalm 23:1, 5 (AMPC):** "The Lord is my Shepherd [to feed, guide, and shield me], I shall not lack.... You prepare a table before me in the presence of my enemies. You anoint my head with oil; my [brimming] cup runs over."

F.   **Psalm 34:10 (AMPC):** "The young lions lack food and suffer hunger, but they who seek (inquire of and require) the Lord [by right of their need and on the authority of His Word], none of them shall lack any beneficial thing."

G.   **Psalm 36:7-9 (AMPC):** "How precious is Your steadfast love, O God! The children of men take refuge and put their trust under the shadow of Your wings. They relish and feast on the abundance of Your own house; and You cause them to drink of the stream of Your pleasures. For with You is the fountain of life; in Your light do we see light." (NLT—the light by which we see)

H. **Psalm 66:12:** "Thou hast caused men to ride over our heads; we went through fire and through water: but thou broughtest us out into a wealthy place."

I. **Psalm 68:19:** "Blessed be the Lord, who daily loadeth us with benefits, even the God of our salvation. Selah."
   1. Psalm 103:2 (AMPC): "Bless (affectionately, gratefully praise) the Lord, O my soul: and forget not [one of] all His benefits."

J. **Psalm 85:12 (AMPC):** "Yes, the Lord will give what is good, and our land will yield its increase."
   1. NLT: "Yes, the Lord pours down His blessings. Our land will yield its bountiful harvest."

K. **Psalm 115:14-15:** "The Lord shall increase you more and more, you and your children. Ye are blessed of the Lord which made heaven and earth."

L. **Malachi 3:10 (AMPC):** "Bring all the tithes (the whole tenth of your income) into the storehouse, that there may be food in My house, and prove Me now by it, says the Lord of hosts, if I will not open the windows of heaven for you and pour you out a blessing, that there shall not be room enough to receive it."

M. **2 Corinthians 9:8-12 (AMPC):** "And God is able to make all grace (every favor and earthly blessing) come to you in abundance, so that you may always and under all circumstances and whatever the need be self sufficient [possessing enough to require no aid or support and furnished in abundance for every good work and charitable donation]. As it is written, He [the benevolent person] scatters abroad; He gives to the poor; His deeds of justice and goodness and kindness and benevolence will go on and endure forever! And [God] who provides [KJV = ministers] seed for the sower and bread for eating will also provide and multiply your [resources for] sowing and increase the fruits of your righteousness [which manifests itself in active goodness, kindness and charity]. Thus you will be enriched in all things and in every way, so that you can be generous and [your generosity as it is] administered by us will bring forth thanksgiving to God. For the service that the ministering of this fund renders does not only fully supply what is lacking to the saints (God's people), but it also overflows in many [cries of] thanksgiving to God."

N. **Philippians 4:19 (AMPC/Greek paraphrase):** My God will liberally supply, fill to the full, cram, furnish, satisfy, finish and complete all of your needs, employment, requirements, lack and business according to His riches, His wealth, His money and His possessions in glory by Christ Jesus.

O. **1 Timothy 6:17 (AMPC):** "As for the rich in this world, charge them not to be proud, arrogant and contemptuous of others, nor to set their hopes on uncertain riches, but on God, Who richly and ceaselessly provides us with everything for [our] enjoyment."

P. **2 Peter 1:3:** "...His divine power hath given unto us all things that pertain unto life and godliness, through the knowledge of him that hath called us to glory and virtue."

OUR COVENANT OF WEALTH
DAY #16

A. **2 Chronicles 16:9:** "For the eyes of the Lord run to and fro throughout the whole earth, to show himself strong in the behalf of them whose heart is perfect toward him."
   1. *Show Himself strong* (HEB) = bestow, grant, extend His covenant wealth
   2. Our covenant with God is His total commitment to support, defend, protect and provide.
   3. God's consuming passion and determination is to locate His covenant people and bless them.
   4. It is an undying covenant devotion that propels Him to extend Himself to us with everything He is and with everything He has.
   5. It is a covenant love that won't give up or quit until the extension of that love is satisfied.
       a. 2 Samuel 9:1-3: David was consumed with locating an heir of Jonathan to bestow covenant wealth upon.
       b. The eyes of David ran to and fro throughout the whole earth searching for an heir of his covenant brother to lavish covenant wealth upon.
       c. How much more is God searching for us!

B. **Deuteronomy 8:18—God Gives Us the Power to Get Wealth in Order to Establish His Covenant With Us and His Covenant on Earth**
   1. NLT: "Remember the Lord your God. He is the one who gives you power to be successful, in order to fulfill the covenant He confirmed to your ancestors with an oath."
   2. Prosperity is a sign of our covenant with God.
   3. Zechariah 8:13 (NLT): "...I will rescue you and will make you both a symbol and a source of blessing."

4. Genesis 17:1-8: God covenanted with Abraham to make him rich.
5. Galatians 3:13-14, 29—We are heirs of the covenant.
    a. Verse 29: "And if ye be Christ's, then are ye Abraham's seed, and heirs according to the promise."

C. "Covenant of Wealth" Scriptures

1. Deuteronomy 28:2: "And all these [covenant] blessings shall come on thee, and overtake thee...."
    a. *Brenton:* "All these blessings shall come upon you and shall find you...."
    b. HEB: "All these blessings shall reach you...."
2. Deuteronomy 28:11: "And the Lord shall make thee plenteous in goods...."
    a. MSG: "God will lavish you with good things...."
    b. AMPC: "He will make you to have a surplus of prosperity...."
3. Ecclesiastes 5:19 (NLT): "And it is a good thing to receive wealth from God and the good health to enjoy it."
4. Genesis 15:1: "Fear not Abram: I am your shield and your exceeding great reward."
    a. AMPC: "I am your Shield, your abundant compensation, and your reward shall be exceedingly great."
    b. HEB: "I am your rapidly increasing money supply."
5. Hebrews 10:35: "Cast not away therefore your confidence, which hath great recompense of reward."
    a. Recompense of reward (GK) MISTHA-PODOSIA
        i. MISTHA = pay, salary, money, repay a debt, payment of wages due
        ii. PODOS = feet
    b. Money is coming on feet in your direction.
    c. "Money cometh to me now!"
6. Psalm 68:19: "Blessed be the Lord, who daily loadeth us with benefits.

    a. *Darby:* "Blessed be the Lord: day by day He loads us with good."

    b. DRB: "Blessed be the Lord day by day: the God of our salvation will make our journey prosperous to us."

7. Psalm 103:2 (AMPC): "Bless the Lord, O my soul, and forget not one of all His (covenant) benefits."

D. What the Word Tells Us About Famine

1. Job 5:20, 22 (NLT): "He will save you from death in time of famine.... You will laugh at destruction and famine."

2. Psalm 33:18-19: "Behold, the eye of the Lord is upon them that fear him, upon them that hope in His mercy [NLT—rely on His unfailing love]; to deliver their soul from death, and to keep them alive in famine."

3. Psalm 37:18-19: Even in famine they will have more than enough.

    a. HEB: He will supply until no more is needed.

4. In famine, we don't just survive—WE THRIVE!

    a. Prosper, flourish, succeed, advance

    b. Grow vigorously

    c. Increase in goods and estate

THE HEART OF PROSPERITY
DAY #20

A. *True Prosperity* **Defined by Kenneth Copeland**
   1. True prosperity is the ability to use the power of God to meet the needs of mankind in every realm of life—spirit, soul, body, financially, socially.
   2. True prosperity is when you make it your need to get salvation into the hands of people and when you make it your purpose to feed the gospel to the unsaved.
   3. True prosperity is the ability to look a man in the eye in his moment of impossibility and take his needs on as your own.
   4. True prosperity is walking with God to be able and equipped to do for others whatever He needs done, whenever He needs it done and with whatever He needs it done.
   5. True prosperity is not for keeping your bills paid and your body well just so you can lie around and watch TV in comfort. God is not prospering us to get us out of debt so we can get into bigger debt. He is not prospering us so we can buy and buy and buy. He is prospering us so we can give and give and give.

B. **Our Motivation for Accumulation Is Distribution**
   1. Genesis 12:2 (AMPC): "I will make of you a great nation, and I will bless you [with abundant increase of favors] and make your name famous and distinguished, and you will be a blessing [dispensing good to others]."
   2. Philippians 2:4: "Look not every man on his own things, but every man also on the things of others."
      a. AMPC: "...Be concerned for not [merely] [your] own interests, but also each for the interests of others."
   3. Galatians 6:10 (KNOX): "Let us practice generosity to all while the opportunity is ours, and above all, to

those who are one family with us in the household of
faith."

    a. Creflo Dollar emptied his entire account and
sowed the money toward KCM's airplane.

    b. He put KCM's need above his own.

    c. Kenneth and Gloria Copeland have sown more
than 30 airplanes, placing others' needs above
their own.

4. 1 Corinthians 10:24: "Let no man seek his own, but
every man another's wealth."

    a. JBP/WOR: Let no man set his own advantage
as his objective, but let each seek the good of
others.

5. "A man's life consists not in the abundance of the
things he possesses, but in the abundance of the things
he sows." —Kenneth Copeland

C. Giving Is at the Very Heart of Prosperity

1. 2 Corinthians 9:11 (NIV): "[As a result of your giv-
ing] you will be enriched in every way so that you can
be generous on every occasion, and through us your
generosity will result in thanksgiving to God."

2. AMPC: "Thus you will be enriched in all things and
in every way, so that you can be generous, and [your
generosity as it is] administered by us will bring forth
thanksgiving to God."

3. Billye Brim shared that during the "Restore Honor"
meeting in Washington, D.C., a rabbi shared that
God's Word commands us to make money because we
are God's stewards on earth with the responsibility to
distribute His wealth.

MY FAITH FOR PROVISION
WORKS ALL THE TIME
DAY #23

A. **Galatians 6:9:** "Let us not be weary in well doing: for in due season we shall reap, if we faint not."
   1. AMPC: "Let us not lose heart and grow weary and faint in acting nobly and doing right, for in due time and at the appointed season we shall reap, if we do not loosen and relax our courage and faint."
   2. A note to Pastor George:
      "Thank you, Pastor George, for teaching us about reaping. We have been going back over your first '10 Days of Prosperity' on the internet. It is really blessing us. We had been asking the same question over and over again—'We tithe and give, but we are not seeing results. Why isn't it working for us?' After reviewing your series, we are very encouraged! Our faith is back on track and is now working again!"
   3. Many ask the same question: "Why isn't it working for me?"
   4. When they tithe and sow and don't see results, they get discouraged, and wonder why it doesn't work.
   5. They don't realize that their harvest is right around the faith corner.

B. **Hebrews 10:23, 35-36:** We Must Stand Firm in Faith Until We See the Results
   1. Verse 23: "Let us hold fast the profession of our faith without wavering; (for he is faithful that promised)."
      a. AMPC: "So let us seize and hold fast and retain without wavering the hope we cherish and confess and our acknowledgement of it, for He Who promised is reliable (sure) and faithful to His word."
      b. NLT: "Let us hold tightly without wavering to the hope we affirm, for God can be trusted to keep his promise."

2. We must stay encouraged and continue to use our faith.
3. Verses 35-36: "Cast not away therefore your confidence, which has great recompense of reward. For ye have need of patience, that, after ye have done the will of God, ye might receive the promise."
    a. AMPC: "Do not, therefore, fling away your fearless confidence, for it carries a great and glorious compensation of reward. For you have need of steadfast patience and endurance, so that you may perform and fully accomplish the will of God, and thus receive and carry away [and enjoy to the full] what is promised."
    b. Cast not away your boldness of speech and confession.
4. Hebrews 6:12: Be imitators of those who through faith and patience inherit the promises.
5. *Patience*
    a. Not knuckling under and hunkering down until the storm passes over
    b. Maintaining your stand in spite of the circumstances
    c. Being constant all the time
    d. The ability to see the results before you have them

C. **Proverbs 18:21: Life and Death Are in the Power of the Tongue**
1. Encourage your faith by speaking life over your tithing and giving.
2. *Tithe*—Declare that the windows of heaven are opened over your life.
3. *Seed*—Declare that your giving is producing an extreme, maximum, overflowing harvest.
4. "My faith is alive, activated and energized."
5. "My faith for provision is working for me all the time!"
    a. Luke 6:38: "I give and it is given to me!"
    b. Galatians 6:7: "I reap what I sow!"
    c. Psalm 112:2: "My seed is mighty upon the earth!"

MONEY COMETH TO ME, NOW!
DAY #25

A. **A Prophetic Word for the Body of Christ From Dr. Leroy Thompson**
1. Dr. Thompson was shopping at the grocery store.
2. While in the checkout line, the person ahead of Dr. Thompson turned to him and said, "Money goes." Dr. Thompson answered, "Money goes."
3. On the way to the car, the Lord corrected him and said, "Money comes."
4. The Lord told him that this was a prophetic word for the Body of Christ.
5. The Lord said we are to declare, "Money cometh to me, now!"

B. **Romans 4:17—We call in things that be not as though they were.**
1. RSV: Call into existence the things that do not exist.
2. *Call* (GK) KALEO = To summon
3. *Summons*—An authoritative command demanding someone to appear
4. Jury duty summons—"You are hereby notified to appear."
5. When you say "Money cometh to me, now," you are actually saying, "Money—you are hereby notified to appear."

C. **Rick Renner's Scriptural Basis for "Money Cometh to Me, Now!"**
1. Rick Renner showed me scriptural proof for "money cometh." (See Rick's handwritten notes attached)
2. Hebrews 10:35: "Cast not away therefore your confidence, which has great recompense of reward."
3. *Recompense of reward* (GK) = MISTHAPODOSIA
   a. MISTHA = Pay, salary, money, recompense, restitution
   b. PODOSIA = Feet or foot (podiatrist)

4. Translations
    a. "Money is coming on feet in your direction."
    b. "Money is traveling your way."
    c. "Money is coming."
5. Provision is running to me
    a. Luke 6:38: "Give, and it shall be given unto you; good measure, pressed down, and shaken together, and running over, shall men give unto your bosom...."
    b. Deuteronomy 28:2: "And all these blessings shall come on thee, and overtake thee...."
    c. Psalm 23:6: "Surely goodness and mercy shall follow me all the days of my life...."
        i. *Follow* (HEB) = Pursue, chase, run after

D. **Confession**

Money, I summon you. I hereby call you to appear. You have feet and you are coming my way. I am a money magnet. Money cometh to me, NOW, in Jesus' Name.

OUR SOURCE OF SUPPLY

DAY #26

A. "What About 2011?"
Word from the Lord through Brother Copeland, November 11, 2010

Now, what about 2011? What is in store? What is God saying about it?

It will be a time of changes. It will be the best of times and it will be the worst of times. The biggest amount of change will come in the harvest. What is harvest to one man is judgment to another one because both of them are the manifestations of seed. Seed grows up and becomes. And when the wages of sin, or the harvest of sin, is death, you just stay with it and it will kill you.

The sower sows the Word. Well, the harvest of that is abundance and plenty—the hundredfold return.

And here is what I heard the Lord say:

For those who insist on compromising the Word and insist on it. I am not talking about the world. I mean, that is what they do all the time. Sinners sin. You understand? That is what they do best. But, I am talking about people who have an allegiance to the Lord Jesus Christ, born-again children of God who continue and insist on compromising the Word.

"Ah, yes, Brother Copeland. I know the Bible says that but you just don't understand my situation." "Ah, yes, Brother Copeland. Yes, I know the Bible says that, but you know, I believe it will be all right with the Lord."

Those who insist and persist in disobedience and the compromising of the Word, whatever you compromise to keep, you will lose it. And the difference is, in 2011, in many cases, it will be taken from you right before your eyes. And of course, it is not God who takes it from you. It is the devil. He is the thief. He comes to steal, kill and destroy. God is not taking things away from you. The devil takes them and blames it on God. He will get preachers to preach that to you, but it isn't true.

Now, for those who insist on keeping the love commandment at any price, and those who insist on living by faith and giving God praise and glory, everything is going to be All-Right. That is what I heard the Lord say. Everything is going to be All-Right. Every thing. All-Right. It is going to right-en up.

Straighten up.

Don't look to the government for your supply. Don't look to other people for your supply. No, no. Pastors, don't look to your congregations for your supply.

Jesus is our Source, hallelujah. The blessing of Abraham is our supply. Praise God!

The Word is our supply. Amen.

Now, to walk in that, oh my goodness. You are going to have to pay attention. You are going to have to listen on purpose. Take time to pray and listen to God.

Jesus said, "I only say those things I hear My Father say, and I only do those things I see My Father do." Note, that should be all of us the same way.

Not what we see someone else do or hear someone else say. We take a message someone preaches. We take the written Word of God as the very Word of Jesus, the very Word of the living God. Amen. It is God speaking to me, but there are moments and times when you need to just hush and quit trying to make up and do all your praying on your own, and be quiet and say, "Sir, what should I say at this moment? What should I do? My ears are open and my eyes are open. I am listening."

B. **Our Source of Supply**
   1. "Don't look to the government for your supply."
   2. "Don't look to other people for your supply."
   3. "Pastors, don't look to your congregations for your supply."
   4. "Jesus is our Source of supply."
   5. "The Blessing of Abraham is our source of supply."
   6. "The Word is our source of supply."

7. "My God is the source of all my supply."
   a. This must be ingrained in our thinking.
   b. Especially during economic times like these

C. Settle This Today: God Is My Source!

1. *Source*—Point of origin
   a. The beginning place
   b. Where something can be traced back to
2. *Supply*—Provision, inventory, stock
3. Our source of supply is the point of origin for the fulfillment of all our needs.
4. Philippians 4:19: "My God shall supply all your need according to His riches in glory by Christ Jesus."
   a. BBE: "My God will give you all you have need of from the wealth of his glory in Christ Jesus."
   b. AMPC: "My God will liberally supply (fill to the full) your every need according to His riches in glory in Christ Jesus."
5. I settle this today:
   a. Jesus is the Source of my supply.
   b. The Blessing of Abraham is the source of my supply.
   c. The Word of God is the source of my supply.
   d. God is the source of my supply!

The Hundredfold Return
DAY #27

A. Mark 10:28-30: He Shall Receive an Hundredfold
(Quotes from Gloria Copeland's book, *God's Will Is Prosperity*)

1. Verses 28-30: "Peter said to him, See, we have given up everything, and come after you. Jesus said, Truly I say to you, There is no man who has given up house, or brothers, or sisters, or mother, or father, or children, or land, because of me and the good news, who will not get a hundred times as much now in this time, houses, and brothers, and sisters, and mothers, and children, and land—though with great troubles; and, in the world to come, eternal life."

2. "How great the hundredfold return is: give $1 and receive $100!"

3. "Where in the natural world are you offered the return of 100 times your investment?"
   a. "If you double your money, you do well."
   b. "If you receive 10 times your investment, it is a marvelous deal."
   c. "But who talks in terms of receiving 100 times your investment?"

4. "After I let what the Word offers us in the hundredfold return become a reality to me, the Lord led me to continually give thanks for it every time I thought about it."
   a. "I would say, 'Thank You, Father, for the hundredfold return offered in Your Word.'"
   b. "It is such a generous return and it belongs to me."

5. "I would say any faith words of praise that came into my spirit in regard to continually thanking God for the hundredfold return."

      a. "This thanksgiving kept my faith active and operative to receive."

      b. "Continually confessing the hundredfold return causes the seed of Mark 10:29-30 to grow."

B. Keep Your Faith Active All the Time

  1. Mark 10:30: Now in this time

      a. GW: Here in this life

  2. "I realized that the hundredfold return is continually working, coming to me as long as I keep my faith active in its behalf."

  3. "None of the blessings of God work automatically, even though they belong to us. They become manifested in our lives as we exercise our faith to receive them."

  4. "Healing belongs to every believer, but that great blessing is enjoyed only by those who exercise their faith to receive it."

  5. "In the same way, the hundredfold return is a powerful force in the believer's financial blessing, but you have to release your faith to receive all that the Word offers you. The force of faith for the hundredfold return must be applied by the Word of God in your heart and by the confession of your mouth."

C. The Hundredfold Return Is Working for Me All the Time!

  1. Kenneth and Gloria had been attending a convention in Hawaii.

  2. On the morning of their departure, Gloria went to the restaurant to get a table.

  3. A man stepped in front of her and took the table that should have been hers.

  4. Gloria ended up having to get a table in the very back of the restaurant.

  5. A woman came up to Gloria and took a ring off her finger, gave it to Gloria and said, "God told me to give this to you. I had been impressed for several days to do

this. I asked the Lord during the meeting that if He wanted me to give Gloria Copeland the ring, please have her sit next to me at breakfast in the morning."

6. The ring was stunning and unusual—two squares of emeralds and diamonds set in gold. The two squares rotated as her hand moved. Gloria received it and prayed for the woman.

7. Then she remembered the hundredfold return. The last time they were in Hawaii, at the very same hotel, the Lord impressed Gloria to give someone a diamond ring. When she gave it, she believed for the hundredfold return. The hundredfold was working for her all along.

8. As Gloria looked at the rotating squares of the ring, the Lord impressed her that this ring was to be a reminder that the hundredfold return is continually working for her all the time.

9. Continually keep your faith activated for the hundredfold return.

10. Continually confess, "The hundredfold return is working for me all the time!"

WHAT IT WILL TAKE
TO PROSPER IN THESE TIMES—
TOTAL IMMERSION
DAY #30

A. **Romans 12:1-2—Do Not Be Conformed to the World**
   1. The attack on the mind is immense.
   2. "How are we going to make it during these times?"
   3. *Conformed*—to shape like another
      a. MSG: Don't become so well-adjusted to your culture that you fit into it without even thinking.
      b. PHI: Don't let the world squeeze you into its mold.
   4. *Transformed*—to undergo a complete change
      a. AMPC: Be transformed—changed by the entire renewal of your mind by its new ideals and its new attitude.
      b. GW: Change the way you think.
      c. PHI: Let God remold your mind from within.
   5. Isaiah 26:3: "Thou wilt keep him in perfect peace, whose mind is stayed on thee: because he trusteth in thee."
      a. NLT: "You will keep in perfect peace all who trust in you, all whose thoughts are fixed on you!"
      b. *Stayed*—established, focused, totally immersed

B. **Psalm 1:1-3—The Principle of Total Immersion**
   1. Verses 1-3: "Blessed is the man that walketh not in the counsel of the ungodly, nor standeth in the way of sinners, nor sitteth in the seat of the scornful. But his delight is in the law of the Lord; and in his law doth he meditate day and night. And he shall be like a tree planted by the rivers of water, that bringeth forth his fruit in his season; his leaf also shall not wither; and whatsoever he doeth shall prosper."

2. "Day and night" is total immersion in God's Word.
3. Total transformation in your thinking comes from total immersion in God's Word.
4. By constantly immersing yourself in God's Word, you will flush out all fear of failure and become rooted in the truth of your prosperity.
5. This is what it will take to break the lack mentality and establish a new way of thinking.

C. My Personal Total Immersion Program
1. Terri and I prayed and believed the Lord wanted us to sow our house debt free.
    a. The pressure of what to do next began to consume my mind.
    b. I found myself living by fear instead of faith.
2. The Lord led me to do three things to totally immerse my thinking and get me back over into faith for prosperity.
3. I totally immersed myself in scriptures that took my limitations off God.
    a. Genesis 18:14: Is anything too hard for the Lord? NO!
    b. Numbers 11:23 (AMPC): Has the Lord's hand, ability and power become short, thwarted and inadequate? NO!
    c. Matthew 19:26: With men, this is impossible. But with God, all things are possible. YES!
4. I totally immersed myself in Dr. Leroy Thompson's audio series *Money Cometh*, and Brother Copeland's audio series *The Laws of Prosperity*.
    a. I listened to them all the time.
    b. At home, in the car, on the plane—everywhere!
5. I totally immersed myself in God's Word by locating and meditating on 21 major ways that God provides along with the total of 191 scripture references. (See list in the previous section.)
    a. My spirit was strengthened.
    b. My faith was fed.

c. My mind was renewed.
d. My life was completely transformed.
e. That is what it will take to prosper in these times.

How to Apply for a Heavenly Grant
DAY #32

A. From *The Laws of Prosperity* CD Series

1. During the very early years of Kenneth and Gloria's ministry, A.W. Copeland, Kenneth's father, was the business administrator and only employee.
2. He came to Kenneth one day and said, "Do you have any idea how much money it takes to operate this ministry?"
3. Brother Copeland replied, "No, and I don't want to know!"
4. His father said, "I think you ought to pray about it. We have grown so much in the last 90 days that I don't think you have any idea what it costs to run this."
5. He laid a piece of paper on Kenneth's desk with a figure on it and then walked away.
   a. Kenneth picked up the paper, looked at it and "almost choked"!
   b. He then said to himself, "Looks like I should do something about this."

B. The Lord Began to Speak

1. "Boy, don't you start that. You know better than that."
2. "You know who your Source of supply is."
3. "You get over there on your knees and you get it that way!"
4. As Brother Copeland began to pray, the Lord told him to look up two scriptures in *The Amplified Bible, Classic Edition*.
   a. John 16:23: "And when that time comes, you will ask nothing of Me [you will need to ask Me no questions]. I assure you, most solemnly I tell you, that My Father will grant you whatever you ask in My Name."
   b. Mark 11:24: "For this reason I am telling you,

whatever you ask for in prayer, believe (trust
and be confident) that it is granted to you, and
you will [get it]."
5. *Grant* defined
   a. A sum of money provided by a government,
   local authority or public fund to finance educa-
   tional study, overseas aid, building repairs, etc.
   b. There are students able to attend college because of a grant.
   c. *To grant*—to give, bestow or confer
   d. A heavenly grant comes from another Source.

C. How to Apply for a Heavenly Grant
1. Brother Copland took the piece of paper his dad gave
   to him and wrote on it
2. "According to John 16:23 (AMPC), I submit this request in the Name of Jesus: I lay claim of my heavenly
   grant of $_____ every 30 days."
3. "According to Mark 11:24 (AMPC), I am confident
   that whatever I ask in prayer, it is granted to me. I
   believe I receive my grant in Jesus' Name."
4. From that moment on, the finances came in.
5. That was 40 years ago—and the bills are still paid in
   full!

D. A Sample Request for a Heavenly Grant
*Be it known this day, _____, we receive a
heavenly grant in the amount of $_____. Father, in
the Name of Jesus, we come boldly to the throne of grace, and
present Your Word.*

*According to John 16:23 (AMPC), Jesus said, "I assure
you, most solemnly I tell you, that My Father will grant you
whatever you ask in My Name."*

*Jesus, You said in Mark 11:24 (AMPC), "Whatever
you ask for in prayer, believe (trust and be confident) that it is
granted to you, and you will [get it]."*

*Your Word states in Luke 6:38, "Give, and it shall be
given unto you; good measure, pressed down, and shaken
together, and running over, shall men give unto your bosom."*

In accordance to Your Word, we give, we sow seed, in order to set this spiritual law to work on our behalf.

According to Matthew 18:18, we bind Satan and all his forces, and render them helpless and unable to operate. They will not hinder our grant.

According to Hebrews 1:13 and 14, we loose the ministering spirits and charge them to go forth and cause our grant to come into our hands.

Jesus, You said in Matthew 18:19, "Again I say unto you, That if two of you shall agree on earth as touching any thing that they shall ask, it shall be done for them of My Father which is in heaven."

Therefore, we set ourselves in agreement, and we believe we receive now, and we praise You for it.

YOU CAN LIVE DEBT FREE—PART 1
DAY #33

A. Matthew 6:33—Seek First the Kingdom of God
1. "Seek ye first the kingdom of God, and his righteousness; and all these things shall be added unto you."
2. AMPC: "But seek, aim at and strive after first of all His kingdom and His righteousness, His way of doing and being right, and then all these things taken together will be given you besides."
3. How do we seek first the kingdom? We give God's Word first place and final authority in our lives.
4. Commit yourself to obey whatever you see in the Word.
5. From *God's Will Is Prosperity* by Gloria Copeland
    a. "Kenneth and I made that very commitment (the commitment to obey whatever they saw in the Word) years ago when we first began to find out how faith works. We agreed then that we would do whatever we saw in God's Word. Without even knowing it, we had placed ourselves in position to receive great financial blessings."
    b. "Our desire was to please God: we were committed to His Word. We didn't know how to believe God for material things. We didn't even know that the instructions in God's Word would always work to our advantage—even in this life."
    c. "When we first learned that God would meet our needs, we were living in Tulsa, Oklahoma, where Kenneth was enrolled in Oral Roberts University. We desired to please God with all of our hearts, and we had moved out in what little faith we knew."
    d. "Financially, times were hard. I really think that we were supernaturally in debt! No matter how

hard we tried, we couldn't get out of debt; we just seemed to get in deeper and deeper. Borrowed money was our source. After we paid the bills, there was no money left for anything else."

e. "Old obligations were left unpaid, and there was threat of a lawsuit. I can remember standing in the checkout line at the grocery store, praying in the spirit, and believing God that I had enough money to pay for the groceries in my basket. Whatever I had in my purse at the time was all we had!"

f. "We didn't know then what we know now about operating in the laws of prosperity. We were just beginning to learn about the integrity of the Word: that you can depend on God's Word in the same way you depend on the word of a doctor, a lawyer or your very best friend."

g. "We know that the Word of God never fails. We committed to do whatever we saw in the Word, no matter what it was."

h. "Then we saw Romans 13:8...."

B. **Romans 13:8—"Owe no man any thing but to love one another."**

1. "Surely God didn't mean that!"

2. "That scripture must mean something else!"

3. AMPC: "Keep out of debt and owe no man anything, except to love one another."

4. "It looked impossible to do anything without borrowing money. We had never considered paying cash for a car. We had never bought furniture. How would we ever have anything? The material possession I wanted most in the world was a home. Pay cash for a house? You must be kidding! Satan would say, 'You will never get it.' We actually did not know that we could receive all these things with our faith."

5. "We had a choice, but not a good one as far as we could tell. We had said, 'We are taking God's Word

literally and whatever we see in it, that is what we will do.' But when we made that commitment, we did not know the Bible said, 'Keep out of debt.'"

C. **From *The Laws of Prosperity* by Kenneth Copeland**
1. "When Gloria and I first began to put the things we were learning into practice, we had nothing around us but problems. I had returned to college at the age of 30 and from there, God called us into a full-time ministry in His service."
2. "We were deeply in debt and lived in surroundings that were very poor. The job God called me to do required that I travel extensively preaching and teaching His Word, but our car was worn out. We had less than nothing. We were thousands of dollars in debt."
3. "God used His Word to set the standards by which we would operate. It had to be by faith or not at all. We made commitments that seemed so hard. We declared that we would never ask any man for anything including money and places to minister."
4. "We pledged ourselves and this ministry to Romans 13:8 that we would never borrow one cent. We would tell our needs only to God and expect what He was teaching us to produce. We prayed, confessed our faith and stood on God's Word when every circumstance spelled absolute doom. God's Word worked!"
5. "Things began to happen for us instead of to us. We began to grow. In eleven months, we were free from debt."

D. **Make a Quality Decision to Live Debt Free**
1. A quality decision
   a. It forever settles the issue.
   b. It is a decision of no retreat and no return.
   c. It is a memorial that settles all future decisions.
2. "The very moment you make the quality decision to live debt free, God sees you debt free."
3. Settle forever
   a. God is my Source—not people.

b. I am not limited to a salary.
c. It is God's will for me to live debt free.

YOU CAN LIVE DEBT FREE—PART 2
DAY #34

A. **Matthew 6:33—Seek First the Kingdom of God**
 1. "Seek ye first the kingdom of God, and his righteousness; and all these things shall be added unto you."
 2. AMPC: "But seek (aim at and strive after) first of all His kingdom and His righteousness (His way of doing and being right), and then all these things taken together will be given you besides."
 3. Kenneth and Gloria Copeland committed themselves to seek the kingdom by:
    a. Giving God's Word first place.
    b. Making God's Word final authority.
    c. Committing to obey whatever they saw in the Word.
 4. Financial times were hard and they were in debt.
 5. And then they saw Romans 13:8.

B. **Romans 13:8—"Owe no man any thing but to love one another."**
 1. AMPC: "Keep out of debt and owe no man anything, except to love one another."
 2. It looked impossible to do, but they did it.
 3. They made a quality decision to live debt free.
 4. A quality decision forever settles the issue, is a decision of no retreat and is a memorial that settles all future decisions.
 5. They settled forever that God was their Source, they were not limited and it was God's will for them to live debt free.

C. **What Kenneth and Gloria Copeland Did to Live Debt Free**
 —From *God's Will Is Prosperity* by **Gloria Copeland**
 1. "We stopped using our charge accounts and began to believe God to get out of debt."

    a.   "Everything we owned was 'buy now, pay later.'"

    b.   "Sometimes it was much later!"

2.   "We set our affections on God's Word."

    a.   "We were determined to walk according to what we saw in the Word."

    b.   "Things didn't come to us in one day. We had to build the Word of God into our spirits and walk in what we knew. We would get some of the Word in us and walk in it; get more Word in us and walk in that; get more Word in us and walk in that. We were involved in the Word almost every waking hour. Television was not interesting to us. Even the world events could not hold our attention."

    c.   "We were committed to the Word regardless and were not willing to borrow money."

3.   "We devoted ourselves to God's Word literally day and night."

    a.   Joshua 1:8 (AMPC): "This book of the law shall not depart out of your mouth, but you shall meditate on it day and night, that you may observe and do according to all that is written in it. For then you shall make your way prosperous, and then you shall deal wisely and have good success."

4.   "It was 11 months from the time that we first decided to believe God to get out of debt until that goal was achieved. During those 11 months, we stood fast on what we knew from God's Word."

5.   From *The Laws of Prosperity* by Kenneth Copeland

    a.   "We figured out how much we owed. I got my checkbook and wrote out the checks that would pay these debts. We laid hands on them and prayed according to Romans 13:8."

    b.   "Father, in the Name of Jesus, I am putting these checks in this desk drawer and am believing You to get us out of this mess. I am looking to You for the money to pay all these debts, in the Name of Jesus."

c. "I did not mail those checks until the money was in the bank!"

d. "We figured to the last penny how much it would take to operate our household abundantly, even allowing for unexpected things. We wrote it down and prayed over it in the Name of Jesus."

e. "I made up my mind to be single-minded from that day forward. In less than 12 months from that day, we did not owe anything!"

TAKE IT!
DAY #40

A. **Joshua 18:1-3**—"How long are ye slack to go to posses the land, which the Lord God of your fathers hath given you?"
1. NLT: "How long are you going to wait before taking possession of the remaining land the Lord, the God of your ancestors, has given to you?"
2. GNT: "How long are you going to wait before you go in and take the land?"
3. MSG: "How long are you going to sit around on your hands, putting off taking possession of the land that God, the God of your ancestors has given you?"
4. *Slack* (HEB)
   a. Postpone, put off and waste time
   b. Slow, sluggish and lazy
5. How long are you going to put off and be spiritually lazy taking what is yours in Christ?

B. **Mark 11:22-24—Faith Takes!**
1. *Faith* (GK) PISTIS = full persuasion and conviction
2. Faith is never passive, retreating or backward.
   a. Hebrews 10:38-39: "The just shall live by faith: but if any man draw back, my soul shall have no pleasure in him. But we are not of them who draw back unto perdition; but of them that believe to the saving of the soul."
3. Faith is an aggressive force.
   a. Faith is always moving forward.
   b. Faith continually reaches for its goal.
   c. Hebrews 11:33: Who through faith they subdued, possessed and conquered kingdoms
4. Mark 11:24: "Believe that ye receive them, and ye shall have them."

        a. (GK) Take it with much force

        b. (GK) Get hold of

        c. (GK) Seize with a grip which cannot be shaken off

5. Matthew 11:12: "From the days of John the Baptist until now the kingdom of heaven suffereth violence, and the violent take it by force."

        a. We take what is ours with the force of faith

        b. To take by force (GK) HARPADZO

           i. Harpoon

          ii. To pull

         iii. "Moby Dick" says it all!

C. Nehemiah 9:21-25—Go In and Take the Land!

1. Verse 24: "So the children went in and possessed the land."

        a. They went in and took it.

2. Verse 25: "And they took strong cities, and a fat [rich, plenteous and wealthy] land, and possessed houses full of all goods, wells digged, vineyards, and oliveyards, and fruit trees in abundance."

3. Verse 25: "So they did eat, and were filled, and became fat [rich, plenteous and wealthy], and delighted themselves in thy great goodness."

4. Jesus paid the price for us to walk in the blessing of Abraham.

5. Take it in Jesus' Name!!

NOW IS NOT THE TIME
TO QUIT TITHING—PART 1
DAY #44

A. Recent Survey Concerning the Economy's Effect on Giving

1. "The economy has changed many aspects of American life. A new research study explores how the charitable landscape has changed over the last two and a half years. The study examines how many Americans have been affected by the economic downturn, how this has influenced their donations and their outlook on economic recovery."

2. "Church giving has declined since the beginning of this year:
   a. 24% have stopped all giving to churches.
   b. 17% have decreased their giving by 20% or less.
   c. 7% have lessened their donations by 20% to 45%.
   d. 17% have reduced their giving by half.
   e. 12% have decreased their giving by more than half."

3. "The study revealed that the number of people who are tithing has also dropped.
   a. The practice of tithing—donating at least 10% of one's income to churches or other charities—has been relatively stable over the past decade, hovering between 5% and 7%.
   b. Currently, the national tithing rate is down to 4% of the adult population."

4. "It is true that many Americans are living on less due to salary reductions, furloughs, loss of jobs or the inability to get a position that matched a previous salary. These are difficult circumstances for anyone to face and could have a legitimate influence on donations."

5. "However, most of the survey indicators focus less on the amount of dollars donated and more on the

205

underlying attitudes and generosity of Americans. Most Americans think of their giving as secondary to their survival. Yet, from a biblical perspective, generosity should be part of the Christian's fundamental response to the downturn."

"Now is not the time to quit tithing!"

B. Malachi 3:10-12—Bring Ye All the Tithes
1. The tithe is the 10 percent of all our income.
2. Tithing is the faith action by which we bring the 10 percent to Jesus—the High Priest of the tithe.
3. The tithe goes to where we are fed so that we can continue to be fed.
4. God uses the 10 percent to reinvest into our spiritual welfare and benefit.
5. Tithing is the only place in the Bible where God says, "Prove Me."

C. Leviticus 27:30, 32—The Tithe Belongs to God
1. Verse 30: All the tithe is holy unto the Lord.
2. Verse 32: "The tenth shall be holy unto the Lord."
3. *Holy* (HEB) = separated from, consecrated to
4. We are to worship God with our tithe.
5. The tithe gives God the opportunity to fulfill His covenant and protect the other 90 percent.
   a. The tithe places us under warranty.
   b. Everything is covered.

D. A.W. Copeland's Testimony About Tithing During the Great Depression
From the August 1980 *Believer's Voice of Victory* Magazine

In looking back over the years, more specifically the years of the Depression, Vinita and I can see how God really took care of us. He kept me in jobs when there were no jobs. Because of our decision to live for Him, He made sure that our every need was met.

Even though the Depression years were hard for many,

we now see how the Lord met our needs and kept us. The Depression never did have any devastating effect on our lives because we knew the Lord.

One of the real keys that kept us going was the fact that we were tithing. Whether we were working for a salary or on the farm, we tithed. When I made Jesus the Lord of my life, I also made Him Lord over everything I had.

We never missed a payment on our home or any of the cars we owned. I just kept on working and we just kept on tithing. We never lacked anything.

NOW IS NOT THE TIME TO QUIT TITHING—PART 2

DAY #45

A. **Now Is Not the Time to Quit Tithing**
1. Recent survey reports that giving and tithing is down.
2. Malachi 3:8-12—The tithe is the 10 percent of our income and tithing is the process of giving it by faith.
3. The tithe goes to where we are spiritually fed so we can continue to be fed.
4. Leviticus 27:30, 32—The tithe belongs to God and He reinvests it for our benefit.
5. "One of the real keys that kept us going was the fact that we were tithing. We never missed a payment. I just kept on working and we just kept on tithing. We never lacked anything." —A.W. Copeland, referring to tithing during the Great Depression

B. **Deuteronomy 26:1-15—The Proper Handling of the Tithe**
1. Tithing is the faith action that sets the covenant of blessing in motion that opens the windows of heaven.
2. Tithing is done with words of faith, prayerfully and by love.
3. Hebrews 3:1, 7:8—Jesus is the High Priest of the tithe.
4. Jesus takes your tithes and presents them to the Father.
5. Deuteronomy 26:15: "Look down from thy holy habitation, from heaven, and bless thy people Israel, and the land which thou hast given us, as thou swarest unto our fathers, a land that floweth with milk and honey."

C. **Proverbs 3:9-10—Tithing Produces the Overflow**
1. "Honour the Lord with thy substance, and with the firstfruits of all thine increase: So shall thy barns be

filled with plenty, and thy presses shall burst out with
new wine."

2. AMPC: "Honor the Lord with your capital and suf-
    ficiency [from righteous labors] and with the firstfruits
    of all your income; so shall your storage places be filled
    with plenty, and your vats shall be overflowing with
    new wine."

3. MSG: "Honor God with everything you own; give
    him the first and the best. Your barns will burst, and
    your wine vats will brim over."

D. A Farmer's Experiment in Tithing

*From a book written in 1940 by a farmer named Perry
Hayden*

Perry Hayden heard his pastor preach a message about
tithing.

He decided to try an experiment to see how much
harvest a seed would produce.

His plan was to sow one cubic inch of wheat—360
kernels. He committed to the Lord that, for a period of six
years, he would tithe 10 percent of the harvest and sow
the rest.

In the first year, it took a 4-foot by 8-foot plot of land
to sow one cubic inch of seed. At harvest time, he scraped
the ground in order to get every kernel of wheat. Every
precious seed counted. The first year produced a fiftyfold
harvest.

He tithed 10 percent.

In the second year, it took 24' x 60' plot of land to sow
the seed from the harvest of the first year.

He tithed 10 percent.

In the third year, it took three-quarters of an acre to sow.

He tithed 10 percent.

In the fourth year, it took 14 acres to sow.

He tithed 10 percent.

In the fifth year, it took 230 acres to sow.

He tithed 10 percent.

By the sixth year, it took over 2600 acres to sow 5,000 bushels.

Three hundred sixty kernels had turned into 55 billion. And the largest yield was only fiftyfold. Perry Hayden made $288,000 in six years compared to the other farmers who only made an average of $21,000.

The experiment worked. God can bless your harvest when you tithe.

How to Believe God for a House
Part 1
DAY #46

A. **Romans 13:8 (AMPC)—Keep Out of Debt**
  1. In 1967, Kenneth and Gloria determined that whatever they saw in God's Word, they would do.
  2. "If faith won't get it, we won't have it. If the Word won't get it, we don't need it."
  3. Then they found Romans 13:8 (AMPC) that says, "Keep out of debt and owe no man anything, except to love one another."
  4. They committed to live debt free.
  5. From *God's Will Is Prosperity* by Gloria Copeland
     a. "The first thing I began to believe God for was a home."
     b. "But what about Romans 13:8? It says that we are to owe no man anything but to love him. How can you believe God for enough money to buy a home?
     c. "This is one area most people think impossible."
     d. "Many have made the statement, 'Surely you don't have to believe for a home without borrowing money!'"

B. **2 Corinthians 9:8 (AMPC)—"I hung my faith on that scripture."**
  1. "Satan told me that there was no way I could have a home without borrowing money for it."
  2. "Believing God was the only way I could have my home."
  3. "Satan would come to me with doubt and unbelief, and tell me that there was no way that we could buy a house without going into debt. When he would do that, I would trust in and continually confess 2 Corinthians 9:8 (AMPC). It gave me the comfort and strength I needed to stand in faith."

4. "And God is able to make all grace (every favor and earthly blessing) come to you in abundance, so that you may always and under all circumstances and what-ever the need be self-sufficient [possessing enough to require no aid or support and furnished in abundance for every good work and charitable donation]."

5. "I hung my faith on that scripture."
   a. "The Word says that He is able to get it to you."
   b. "Don't look to your job."
   c. "Keep your eye single on the Word."
   d. "He is able to get things done."

C. James 1:5-8—Stay Single-Minded on the Word

1. "When I believe God for something, I don't waver."
2. "I have made a quality decision that the Word is true."
3. "I have built into myself a reliance on God's Word."
4. "I believe His Word more than I believe what I can see or feel."
5. "As I have heard Kenneth Hagin say, 'If you are deter-mined to stand forever, it won't take very long.'"
   a. "That's the way I am when I am believing God for something."
   b. "I could stand forever if necessary."

HOW TO BELIEVE GOD FOR A HOUSE
PART 2
DAY #47

A. Deuteronomy 6:10-11 (AMPC)—Houses Full of All Good Things
1. "We began believing God for the perfect home when we lived in Tulsa, Okla., in 1968."
2. "At the same time, there was a lady in Fort Worth, Texas, who started building her home."
3. "It was several years before I saw that home, but the floor plan was exactly what we needed to meet our needs as a family. It was perfect for us."
4. "She began to build it at the very time we began to believe for it."
5. "God started to work immediately."

B. Every Step Is a Step of Faith
1. "We leased the house for one year and agreed to pay cash for it at the end of that year."
2. "We lived well. But as far as having that much money in cash, we just didn't have it. In the natural there was no reason to expect to have it, but in the spirit we knew our God was able."
3. "When we moved in, the house was in need of repair. It needed to be completely remodeled, so I was faced with a decision."
   a. "I had enough money to start the remodeling."
   b. "This is not our house legally. It would be unwise to put thousands of dollars into a house that doesn't even belong to us."
4. "As an act of faith, I went to work."
5. "When Satan would say, 'That sure is a lot of money for you to lose,' I would answer, 'No, in the Name of Jesus. This is my house and it will be paid for in July. We will pay cash for it and I believe I have the money in the Name of Jesus!'"

C. **Galatians 3:13-14—The Revelation of Divine Prosperity**
1. "Our commitment years before to stay out of debt made the difference."
2. "If we had not committed to God's Word then, we would not know what we know today about God's system of finance."
3. "One day as I was standing in my house, looking out the window and thinking about these things, God gave me what I would call a revelation of divine prosperity."
    a. "Divine prosperity works exactly the same way as divine healing."
    b. "We would allow symptoms of lack to come on us and stay there. We were willing to tolerate them."
    c. "I realized that Jesus bore the curse of poverty at the same time He bore the curse of sickness."
4. "You can believe for divine prosperity just as you believe for divine health. Both blessings already belong to you. You should refuse lack just as quickly as you refuse sickness."
5. "If you make up your mind—make a quality decision—that you are not willing to live in lack, but that you are willing to live in divine prosperity and abundance, Satan cannot stop the flow of God's financial blessings."

HOW TO BELIEVE GOD FOR A HOUSE
PART 3
DAY #48

A. **Galatians 3:13-14—The Revelation of Divine Prosperity**
   1. Kenneth and Gloria were leasing a house, believing God to buy it at the end of a year.
   2. The Lord began to give Gloria revelations of how to believe God for her house.
   3. The first revelation was a revelation of divine prosperity.
   4. The Lord showed her that she was to stand in faith for her prosperity in the same way that she would stand in faith for her healing.
   5. "You begin to walk in divine prosperity with a decision to no longer allow Satan to put symptoms of lack on you."

B. **Isaiah 53:5, 48:17-18—The Revelation of Peace and Prosperity**
   1. Isaiah 53:5: "The chastisement of our peace was upon him."
   2. Isaiah 48:17-18 (AMPC): "Thus says the Lord, your Redeemer, the Holy One of Israel: I am the Lord your God, Who teaches you to profit, Who leads you in the way that you should go. Oh, that you had hearkened to My commandments! Then your peace and prosperity would have been like a flowing river, and your righteousness [the holiness and purity of the nation] like the [abundant] waves of the sea."
   3. Genesis 15:1, AMPC: "Peace and well-being include a prosperous life. God told Abram, 'Fear not, Abram, I am your Shield, your abundant compensation, and your reward shall be exceedingly great.'"
      a. Abundant compensation is far-reaching.
      b. Abundant compensation means everything.
      c. It enveloped Abraham in a blanket of well-being.

215

4. Peace and prosperity go hand in hand. Your prosperity has already been provided for you. Prosperity is yours.
5. *Peace* (HEB) = nothing missing, nothing broken

C. **Genesis 1:26-28—The Revelation of Dominion and Authority**

1. Divine prosperity and abundance belong to you now.
2. We, as born-again believers, have the same authority over the earth that Adam had in the Garden of Eden.
3. Verse 28 (AMPC): "And God blessed them and said to them, Be fruitful, multiply, and fill the earth, and subdue it [using all its vast resources...]."
4. "While we were standing in faith for the money to pay for our house, the Lord reminded me of this scripture and revealed to me that every material thing here came from the earth's vast resources. Every piece of lumber, brick, glass, concrete, mortar—there was nothing in the makeup of our house that had not come from the earth's resources."
   a. "I wasn't taking authority over something that belonged to someone else. That house was up for sale."
   b. "The people had relinquished their authority when they put it on the market."
   c. "I had the right to take authority over it and receive it as mine in the Name of Jesus."
5. "I began to see that I already had authority over that house and authority over the money I needed to purchase it. I said, 'In the Name of Jesus, I take authority over the money I need. I command you to come to me. I take my place and I take dominion over that which I need. I command it to come in Jesus' Name. Ministering spirits, you go and cause it to come.'"

JUST HOW FAR WILL YOU GO ON THE WORD?

A Partner Letter by Kenneth Copeland

Dear Partner,

Mark 4:20:

And these are they which are sown on good ground; such as hear the word, and receive it, and bring forth fruit, some thirtyfold, some sixty, and some an hundred.

Jesus was teaching on the sower soweth the Word. The object of His teaching was how to produce a hundredfold in this life by using God's Word. Notice in verse 20 it says, "...some thirtyfold, some sixty, and some an hundred." Why did some produce more than others? Were the people who produced a hundredfold better ground than those who only brought forth thirty- or sixtyfold? No. The Word says they were all good ground. We know that God is no respecter of persons, so He didn't just decide to bless one more than the other. They all heard the Word and received it. Something had to make the difference.

We hear people say things like, "Well, you know, these things are just not meant to work for some as well as they do for others." Of course, the person who thinks that way always places himself in the category with those who it does not work as well for.

If we read the rest of Jesus' teaching through verse 32, we find that the seed, or the Word, is what produces. Once we see this, it is obvious that the amount of production is in direct relation to the amount of seed sown. Remember, we are not talking about sowing in bad ground. We have already come past that. We are talking about different levels of production in good ground.

Ask yourself these questions: "Just how far will I go on the Word? Where is my compromise point?" The Word says in Ephesians 6: "Having done all, to stand."

Many people ask me if I believe it is a sin to borrow money. The answer is no. It is no more a sin to go to a banker than to go to a doctor. Of course, there are instances that it would be sin—to borrow knowing you can't pay it back is sin.

When God told Israel that He would make them plenteous in goods and they would lend to many and borrow from none, He meant He would supply them better than if they went to another nation.

The point I want to make is this. When Gloria and I decided to owe no man anything, we made that decision to glorify God and please God by walking by faith. We started by making the quality decision to borrow no more and released our faith to pay all the debts we owed. We were faced with believing for our everyday supply.

We learned to believe for the small things first. As God taught us to prosper, the day came when we knew we were ready to have a home. We were faced with the same question I told you to ask yourself. How far will we go on the Word? We made the decision then that if we ever had a choice, we would use our faith instead of some other source.

It took nearly eight years to get that house by faith. We were in a good enough financial position to have borrowed the money and lived in a better house than the one we were living in all those eight years. Believe me, the faith way was better.

We have the perfect home. It is not just a nice home. It became ours through God working miracles. We began by producing thirtyfold. We grew to sixtyfold. We have grown in this area to a hundredfold on God's Word. Each time before we grew, we were faced with the same question: How far will I go? The Word is strong enough in any situation we are ever faced with to go all the way.

Once the decision is made to increase our capacity for faith and grow in any area, we must then begin to meditate the Word in that area. Give the Holy Spirit the opportunity to teach us and train us in what we need to know in order to produce the hundredfold.

Then came confession. The words of our mouths must continually confess the Word that we are meditating. We must not tolerate any thoughts or actions that do not correspond to what we are meditating and confessing. Having done all to stand, stand therefore, forever if necessary. The growth will come.

You will not only be blessed with the manifestation of what you have believed for, but you will be filled with the joy of knowing your Father is pleased—which is far greater than any physical manifestation of any kind. You hear His voice deep in your spirit saying, "Well done, good and faithful servant."

Jesus Is Lord,

Kenneth Copeland

HOW TO BELIEVE GOD FOR A HOUSE—PART 4
DAY #49

A. Ephesians 6:13-14—The Stand of Faith
1. "It was six years from the time we started believing God for the perfect home until we moved into the home we live in now."
2. "At the end of the year's lease, we paid cash for our 'faith house.'"
3. "I am still not sure how, except by faith in God's Word."
4. "Had we borrowed the money, we would still have 35 years to pay!"
5. "Thank God, borrowed money is not our source— HE IS!"

B. This Must Become a Revelation to You
1. "You cannot receive these things just because I tell you about them."
2. "They must become real to you."
3. "You have to take the scriptures on prosperity and meditate on them until they become a reality in your heart, until you know that prosperity belongs to you."
4. "Once you have a revelation of divine prosperity in your spirit, you won't allow Satan to take it from you."
5. "The Word of God is the source of your prosperity."

C. Excerpt From a Partner Letter by Kenneth Copeland
1. Ask yourself: "Just how far will I go on the Word?"
2. "Many people ask me if I believe it is a sin to borrow money. The answer is no. It is no more a sin to go to a banker than to go to a doctor. Of course, there are instances it would be sin—to borrow knowing you can't pay it back is sin. When God told Israel that He would make them plenteous in goods and they would lend to many nations and borrow from none, He meant He would supply them better than if they went to another nation."

3. "When Gloria and I decided to owe no man anything, we made that decision to glorify God and please God by walking by faith. We started by making the quality decision to borrow no more and released our faith to pay all the debts we owed. We were faced with believing for our everyday supply. We learned to believe for the small things first."

4. "As God taught us to prosper, the day came when we knew we were ready to have a home. We were faced with the same question I told you to ask yourself. How far will we go on the Word? We made the decision then if we ever had a choice we would use our faith instead of some other source."

5. "It took the most part of eight years to get that house by faith. We were in a good enough financial position to have borrowed the money and lived in a better house than the one we were living in all of those eight years. Believe me, the faith way was better. We have the perfect home. It is not just a nice home.... The Word is strong enough in any situation."

D. Seven House Scriptures

1. Proverbs 24:3-4: "Through wisdom is an house builded and by understanding it is established: And by knowledge shall the chambers be filled with all precious and pleasant riches."

2. Proverbs 15:6: "In the house of the righteous is much treasure."

3. 1 Kings 6:38: "The house [was] finished throughout all the parts thereof."

4. Proverbs 12:7: "The house of the righteous shall stand."

5. Proverbs 3:33: "[God] blesseth the habitation of the just."

6. Hebrews 11:10: "[The] builder and maker is God."

7. Ephesians 2:21: "The building [is] fitly framed together."

SYMBOLS OF KINGDOM PROSPERITY
DAY #59

A. **Genesis 26:26-29—Prosperity Can Be Seen**
1. Verse 28 (NIV/NLT): We can clearly and plainly see that the Lord is with you.
2. Verse 28 (MSG): "We've realized that God is on your side."
3. Verse 29 (GNB): "Now it is clear that the Lord has blessed you."

B. **Symbols of Kingdom Prosperity**
1. Zechariah 8:13 (NLT-96): "Among the nations, Judah and Israel had become symbols of what it means to be cursed. But no longer! *Now, I will rescue you and make you both a symbol and a source of blessing.* So don't be afraid or discouraged, but instead, get on with rebuilding the temple."
2. Zechariah 9:16-17: "And the Lord their God shall save them in that day as the flock of his people: for they shall be as the stones of a crown, lifted up as an ensign upon his land. For how great is his goodness, and how great is his beauty! corn shall make the young men cheerful, and new wine the maids."
   a. *Lifted up* (HEB) = Conspicuous, sparkle
   b. *Ensign* (HEB) = To gleam from afar, to be conspicuous as a signal, a flag fluttering in the wind, a sign, a banner, a token, an emblem
   c. NKJV: "The Lord their God will save them in that day, as the flock of His people: For they shall be like the jewels of a crown, lifted up like a banner over His land."
   d. GW: "On that day the Lord their God will rescue them as the flock of his people. They will certainly sparkle in his land like jewels in a crown."

3. Psalm 67:7 (MSG): "God! Let people thank and enjoy you. Let all people thank and enjoy you. Earth, display your exuberance! You mark us with blessing, O God, our God. You mark us with blessing, O God."

4. Genesis 12:2-3 (AMPC): "I will make of you a great nation, and I will bless you [with abundant increase of favors] and make your name famous and distinguished, and you will be a blessing [dispensing good to others]. ...in you will all the families and kindred of the earth be blessed [and by you they will bless themselves]."

5. Deuteronomy 28:10-11 (AMPC): "And all people of the earth shall see that you are called by the name [and in the presence of] the Lord, and they shall be afraid of you. And the Lord shall make you have a surplus of prosperity."

   a. MSG: "All the peoples on Earth will see you living under the Name of God and hold you in respectful awe. God will lavish you with good things: children from your womb, offspring from your animals, and crops from your land, the land that God promised your ancestors that he would give you."

6. Jeremiah 33:9 (NLT): "Then this city will bring me joy, glory, and honor before all the nations of the earth! The people of the world will see all the good I do for my people, and they will tremble with awe at the peace and prosperity I provide for them."

7. Philippians 2:15-16 (AMPC): "That you may show yourselves to be blameless and guiltless, innocent and uncontaminated, children of God without blemish (faultless, unrebukable) in the midst of a crooked and wicked generation [spiritually perverted and perverse], among whom you are seen as bright lights (stars or beacons shining out clearly) in the [dark] world, holding out [to it] and offering [to all men] the Word of Life, so that in the day of Christ I may have something of which exultantly to rejoice and glory in that

I did not run my race in vain or spend my labor to no
purpose."

C. Genesis 26:32—Isaac's Servants Hit a Gusher!

1. They struck a massive underground river.
2. Even in a time of drought, there is always more than
   enough.
3. Kingdom prosperity works anytime, anywhere, under
   any circumstance.

THE FULL SCOPE OF PROSPERITY
DAY #62

A. **3 John 2:** "Beloved, I wish above all things that thou mayest prosper and be in health, even as thy soul prospereth."
   1. *Prosperity* (GK) = help along the way; a prosperous journey
   2. To prosper is to succeed at everything we do.
      a. AMPC: "Beloved, I pray that you may prosper in every way and [that your body] may keep well, even as [I know] your soul keeps well and prospers."
      b. BBE: "My loved one, it is my prayer that you may do well in all things, and be healthy in body, even as your soul does well."
      c. WNT: "My dear friend, I pray that you may in all respects prosper and enjoy good health, just as your soul already prospers."
   3. Prosperity is more than money—it encompasses the entire scope and spectrum of our lives.
   4. Ephesians 1:3: "Blessed be the God and Father of our Lord Jesus Christ, who hath blessed us with all spiritual blessings in heavenly places in Christ."
   5. 2 Peter 1:2-4: "Grace and peace be multiplied unto you through the knowledge of God, and of Jesus our Lord, according as his divine power hath given unto us all things that pertain unto life and godliness, through the knowledge of him that hath called us to glory and virtue: whereby are given unto us exceeding great and precious promises: that by these ye might be partakers of the divine nature, having escaped the corruption that is in the world through lust."

B. **Whatever We Do Shall Prosper**
   1. Psalm 1:1-3: "Blessed is the man that walketh not in the counsel of the ungodly, nor standeth in the way of

sinners, nor sitteth in the seat of the scornful. But his delight is in the law of the Lord; and in his law doth he meditate day and night. And he shall be like a tree planted by the rivers of water, that bringeth forth his fruit in his season; his leaf also shall not wither; and whatsoever he doeth shall prosper."

2. Deuteronomy 29:9: "Keep therefore the words of this covenant, and do them, that ye may prosper in all that ye do."

3. Genesis 39—Everything Joseph did prospered.
   a. Verse 2: "The Lord was with Joseph, and he was a prosperous man...."
   b. Verse 3: "...The Lord made all that he did to prosper in his hand."
   c. Verse 5: "...The blessing of the Lord was upon all that he had in the house, and in the field."
   d. Verse 23: "...That which he did, the Lord made it to prosper."

4. Psalm 112—The profile of a prosperous believer

5. Joshua 1:7-8 (NKJV): "Be strong and very courageous, that you may observe to do according to all the law which Moses My servant commanded you: do not turn from it to the right hand or to the left, that you may prosper wherever you go. This Book of the Law shall not depart from your mouth, but you shall meditate in it day and night, that you may observe to do according to all that is written in it. For then you will make your way prosperous, and then you will have good success."

C. Prosperity includes success in every realm of life—spirit, soul, body, financial, relational, political.
   1. Spiritual prosperity
      a. Born again and spirit filled
      b. Fellowship with the Father
      c. Working with the Father in prayer
      d. Effective soul winner
      e. Revelation of the Word

2. Prosperity of the soul—mind, will, emotions
   a. Peace in your mind
   b. Alignment of your will to God's will
   c. Stability in your emotions
3. Physical prosperity
   a. Living in divine health
   b. Protection
   c. Fear free
4. Financial prosperity
   a. Increase and abundance
   b. Bills paid
   c. Debt freedom
   d. Success in all endeavors
5. Relational prosperity
   a. Love in your home
   b. Devotion in marriage
   c. Obedient children
   d. Healthy relationships
   e. Friends
6. Political prosperity
   a. A God-fearing nation
   b. Godly leadership
   c. Support for Israel

DAYS OF PROSPERITY

THE PROFILE OF A WEALTHY BELIEVER
DAY #90

Foundation Scripture: "Charge them that are rich in this world, that they be not highminded, nor trust in uncertain riches, but in the living God, who giveth us richly all things to enjoy; that they do good, that they be rich in good works, ready to distribute, willing to communicate; laying up in store for themselves a good foundation against the time to come, that they may lay hold on eternal life" (1 Timothy 6:17-19).

A. 1 Timothy 6:17-19—Be Ready and Willing to Give
1. Paul knew that the rich had a tendency toward being tightfisted with their money.
2. He had to instruct them to be ready and willing to give.
   a. Give to God with their tithe.
   b. Give to the ministry with their offering.
   c. Give to others with their harvest.
      i. Ephesians 4:28: "Let him that stole steal no more: but rather let him labour, working with his hands the thing which is good, that he may have to give to him that needeth."
3. *Ready to distribute* (GK) = liberal in giving; generous
   a. MSG: "Be extravagantly generous."
   b. AMPC: "Be liberal and generous of heart."
4. *Willing to communicate* (GK) = an eagerness to share with others
   a. WNT: Openhanded
   b. Given freely and cheerfully
5. 2 Corinthians 9:7 (AMPC): "Let each one [give] as he has made up his own mind and purposed in his heart, not reluctantly or sorrowfully or under compulsion, for God loves (He takes pleasure in, prizes above other things, and is unwilling to abandon or to do without)

a cheerful (joyous, "prompt to do it") giver [whose heart is in his giving]."

B. Psalm 112—The Profile of a Wealthy Believer

1. Verse 1—He is blessed because he honors God and His Word.
   a. To be blessed is to be empowered to prosper.
   b. To be blessed is also to be a blessing.
   c. Genesis 12:2 (AMPC): "And I will make of you a great nation, and I will bless you [with abundant increase of favors] and make your name famous and distinguished, and you will be a blessing [dispensing good to others]."
   d. Zechariah 8:13 (NLT): "Among the other nations, Judah and Israel became symbols of a cursed nation. But no longer! Now I will rescue you and make you both a symbol and a source of blessing."
2. Verse 2—His children are blessed because of his giving.
   a. NLT: "Their children will be successful everywhere; an entire generation of godly people will be blessed."
   b. Psalm 25:12-13 (NIV-84): "Who, then, is the man that fears the Lord? He will instruct him in the way chosen for him. He will spend his days in prosperity, and his descendants will inherit the land."
   c. Psalm 37:25 (NIV-84): "I was young and now I am old, yet I have never seen the righteous forsaken or their children begging bread. They are always generous and lend freely; their children will be blessed."
   d. Psalm 128:1-3 (NIV-84): "Blessed are all who fear the Lord, who walk in his ways. You will eat the fruit of your labor; blessings and prosperity will be yours. Your wife will be like a fruitful vine within your house; your sons will be like olive shoots around your table."

3. Verse 3—Wealth and riches are in his house.
   a. NLT: "They themselves will be wealthy, and their good deeds will last forever."
   b. MSG: "Their houses brim with wealth and a generosity that never runs dry."
4. Verse 4—He is gracious and full of compassion.
   a. *Compassion* (HEB) = a moving, a deep inner yearning, an overwhelming desire of the heart toward supplying the needs of others
   b. Compassion is God's love surging through the heart of one to another.
   c. Luke 10:33-35: "But a certain Samaritan, as he journeyed, came where he was: and when he saw him, he had compassion on him, and went to him, and bound up his wounds, pouring in oil and wine, and set him on his own beast, and brought him to an inn, and took care of him. And on the morrow when he departed, he took out two pence, and gave them to the host, and said unto him, Take care of him; and whatsoever thou spendest more, when I come again, I will repay thee."
5. Verse 5—He displays favor and lends.
   a. MSG: "The good person is generous and lends lavishly."
   b. NIV-84: "Good will come to him who is generous and lends freely, who conducts his affairs with justice."
   c. Proverbs 11:24-25 (NIV-84): "One man gives freely, yet gains even more; another withholds unduly, but comes to poverty. A generous man will prosper; he who refreshes others will himself be refreshed."
   d. Philemon 1:18-19: "If he hath wronged thee, or oweth thee ought, put that on mine account; I Paul have written it with mine own hand, I will repay it: albeit I do not say to thee how thou owest unto me even thine own self besides."

6. Verses 6-8—His heart is established and is not moved during adverse economic times.
    a. Jeremiah 17:7-8 (AMPC): "[Most] blessed is the man who believes in, trusts in, and relies on the Lord, and whose hope and confidence the Lord is. For he shall be like a tree planted by the waters that spreads out its roots by the river; and it shall not see and fear when heat comes; but its leaf shall be green. It shall not be anxious and full of care in the year of drought, nor shall it cease yielding fruit."
    b. Psalm 1:3 (NIV-84): "He is like a tree planted by streams of water, which yields its fruit in season and whose leaf does not wither. Whatever he does prospers."
7. Verse 9—He is a giver who reaches out to the poor and continues to be promoted.
    a. AMPC: "He has distributed freely [he has given to the poor and needy]."
        i. Our motivation for accumulation is distribution.
    b. MSG: "They lavish gifts on the poor—a generosity that goes on, and on, and on. An honored life! A beautiful life!"
    c. Proverbs 19:17: "He that hath pity upon the poor lendeth unto the Lord; and that which he hath given will he pay him again."
    d. Proverbs 22:9 (NIV-84): "A generous man will himself be blessed, for he shares his food with the poor."
    e. Proverbs 31:20 (NIV): "She opens her arms to the poor and extends her hands to the needy."
8. Verse 10—He resists the devil—and the devil flees!
    a. Lack of any kind has no place in the house of the righteous.
    b. The prosperous believer stands strong and firm.

C. **1 Timothy 6:19—A Foundation for the Future**
1. By following these instructions, the rich will be laying up in store for themselves a good foundation against the time to come, that they may lay hold on eternal life.
2. *Laying up in store* (GK)
   a. To treasure away
   b. To store up a treasury
   c. To deposit in abundance for future use
3. *A good foundation* (GK)
   a. Something put down
   b. The foundation of a building, wall or a city
   c. The beginnings, the first principals, system of truth
4. That they may lay hold on eternal life
   a. Not just for heaven
   b. Eternal life is also the quality of life here and now.
5. Matthew 6:20-21 (NIV-84): "But store up for your-selves treasures in heaven, where moth and rust do not destroy, and where thieves do not break in and steal. For where your treasure is, there your heart will be also."

D. **Are You Prepared for Prosperity?**
"...I am looking to and fro across the earth for those to whom I may show Myself strong and transfer My property and My influence in the earth out of the hands of the powers of darkness and into the hands of My people.

"Are you prepared?

"What would you do if I put you in charge?

"Would you follow the plan that the world already has that is full of confusion and doubt and unbelief, or would you dare rise up and say, 'Thus saith The LORD...'?"

—Word from the Lord through Kenneth Copeland, June 27, 2011

THE BLESSING
OF ABRAHAM
DEUTERONOMY
28 : 1 - 14

1   And it shall come to pass, if thou shalt hearken diligently unto the voice of the Lord thy God, to observe and to do all his commandments which I command thee this day, that the Lord thy God will set thee on high above all nations of the earth:

2   And all these blessings shall come on thee, and overtake thee, if thou shalt hearken unto the voice of the Lord thy God.

3   Blessed shalt thou be in the city, and blessed shalt thou be in the field.

4   Blessed shall be the fruit of thy body, and the fruit of thy ground, and the fruit of thy cattle, the increase of thy kine, and the flocks of thy sheep.

5   Blessed shall be thy basket and thy store.

6   Blessed shalt thou be when thou comest in, and blessed shalt thou be when thou goest out.

7   The Lord shall cause thine enemies that rise up against thee to be smitten before thy face: they shall come out against thee one way, and flee before thee seven ways.

8   The Lord shall command the blessing upon thee in thy storehouses, and in all that thou settest thine hand unto; and he shall bless thee in the land which the Lord thy God giveth thee.

9 The Lord shall establish thee an holy people unto himself, as he hath sworn unto thee, if thou shalt keep the commandments of the Lord thy God, and walk in his ways.

10 And all people of the earth shall see that thou art called by the name of the Lord; and they shall be afraid of thee.

11 And the Lord shall make thee plenteous in goods, in the fruit of thy body, and in the fruit of thy cattle, and in the fruit of thy ground, in the land which the Lord sware unto thy fathers to give thee.

12 The Lord shall open unto thee his good treasure, the heaven to give the rain unto thy land in his season, and to bless all the work of thine hand: and thou shalt lend unto many nations, and thou shalt not borrow.

13 And the Lord shall make thee the head, and not the tail; and thou shalt be above only, and thou shalt not be beneath; if that thou hearken unto the commandments of the Lord thy God, which I command thee this day, to observe and to do them:

14 And thou shalt not go aside from any of the words which I command thee this day, to the right hand, or to the left, to go after other gods to serve them.

Prayer for Salvation and Baptism
in the Holy Spirit

Heavenly Father, I come to You in the Name of Jesus. Your Word says, "Whosoever shall call on the name of the Lord shall be saved" (Acts 2:21). I am calling on You. I pray and ask Jesus to come into my heart and be Lord over my life according to Romans 10:9-10: "If thou shalt confess with thy mouth the Lord Jesus, and shalt believe in thine heart that God hath raised him from the dead, thou shalt be saved. For with the heart man believeth unto righteousness; and with the mouth confession is made unto salvation." I do that now. I confess that Jesus is Lord, and I believe in my heart that God raised Him from the dead. I repent of sin. I renounce it. I renounce the devil and everything he stands for. Jesus is my Lord.

I am now reborn! I am a Christian—a child of Almighty God! I am saved! You also said in Your Word, "If ye then, being evil, know how to give good gifts unto your children: HOW MUCH MORE shall your heavenly Father give the Holy Spirit to them that ask him?" (Luke 11:13). I'm also asking You to fill me with the Holy Spirit. Holy Spirit, rise up within me as I praise God. I fully expect to speak with other tongues as You give me the utterance (Acts 2:4). In Jesus' Name. Amen!

Begin to praise God for filling you with the Holy Spirit. Speak those words and syllables you receive—not in your own language, but the language given to you by the Holy Spirit. You have to use your own voice. God will not force you to speak. Don't be concerned with how it sounds. It is a heavenly language!

Continue with the blessing God has given you and pray in the spirit every day.

You are a born-again, Spirit-filled believer. You'll never be the same!

Find a good church that boldly preaches God's Word and obeys it. Become part of a church family who will love and care for you as you love and care for them.

We need to be connected to each other. It increases our strength in God. It's God's plan for us.

Make it a habit to watch the Believer's Voice of Victory Network and become a doer of the Word, who is blessed in his doing (James 1:22-25).

About the Author

Gloria Copeland is a noted author and minister of the gospel whose teaching ministry is known throughout the world. Believers worldwide know her through Believers' Conventions, Victory Campaigns, magazine articles, teaching audios and videos, and the daily and Sunday *Believer's Voice of Victory* television broadcast, which she hosts with her husband, Kenneth Copeland. She is known for Healing School, which she began teaching and hosting in 1979 at KCM meetings. Gloria delivers the Word of God and the keys to victorious Christian living to millions of people every year.

Gloria is author of the New York Times best-seller, *God's Master Plan for Your Life* and *Live Long, Finish Strong*, as well as numerous other favorites, including *God's Will for You, Walk With God, God's Will Is Prosperity, Hidden Treasures* and *To Know Him*. She has also co-authored several books with her husband, including *Family Promises, Healing Promises* and the best-selling daily devotionals, *From Faith to Faith* and *Pursuit of His Presence*.

She holds an honorary doctorate from Oral Roberts University. In 1994, Gloria was voted Christian Woman of the Year, an honor conferred on women whose example demonstrates outstanding Christian leadership. Gloria is also the co-founder and vice president of Kenneth Copeland Ministries in Fort Worth, Texas.

Learn more about Kenneth Copeland Ministries
by visiting our website at **kcm.org**

Materials to Help You
Receive Your Healing
by Gloria Copeland

Books

* And Jesus Healed Them All
* God's Prescription for Divine Health
* God's Will for Your Healing
* Harvest of Health

Words That Heal (gift book with CD enclosed)

Audio Resources

Be Made Whole—Live Long, Live Healthy

God Wants You Well

Healing Confessions (CD and minibook)

Healing School

DVD Resources

Be Made Whole—Live Long, Live Healthy

Know Him As Healer

*Available in Spanish

When The LORD first spoke to Kenneth and Gloria Copeland about starting the *Believer's Voice of Victory* magazine...

He said: *This is your seed. Give it to everyone who ever responds to your ministry, and don't ever allow anyone to pay for a subscription!*

For more than 50 years, it has been the joy of Kenneth Copeland Ministries to bring the good news to believers. Readers enjoy teaching from ministers who write from lives of living contact with God, and testimonies from believers experiencing victory through God's WORD in their everyday lives.

Today, the *BVOV* magazine is mailed monthly, bringing encouragement and blessing to believers around the world. Many even use it as a ministry tool, passing it on to others who desire to know Jesus and grow in their faith!

Request your FREE subscription to the *Believer's Voice of Victory* magazine today!

Go to **freevictory.com** to subscribe online, or call us at **1-800-600-7395** (U.S. only) or **+1-817-852-6000**.

We're Here for You!®

Your growth in God's WORD and victory in Jesus are at the very center of our hearts. In every way God has equipped us, we will help you deal with the issues facing you, so you can be the **victorious overcomer** He has planned for you to be.

The mission of Kenneth Copeland Ministries is about all of us growing and going together. Our prayer is that you will take full advantage of all The LORD has given us to share with you.

Wherever you are in the world, you can watch the *Believer's Voice of Victory* broadcast on television (check your local listings), the Internet at kcm.org or on our digital Roku channel.

Our website, **kcm.org,** gives you access to every resource we've developed for your victory. And, you can find contact information for our international offices in Africa, Australia, Canada, Europe, Ukraine and our headquarters in the United States.

Each office is staffed with devoted men and women, ready to serve and pray with you. You can contact the worldwide office nearest you for assistance, and you can call us for prayer at our U.S. number, 1-817-852-6000, seven days a week!

We encourage you to connect with us often and let us be part of your everyday walk of faith!

Jesus Is LORD!

Kenneth & Gloria Copeland

Kenneth and Gloria Copeland